GOLF'S WINNING STROKE: *Putting*

Golf's Winning

By TOM MICHAEL and the

Stroke: *PUTTING*

Editors of *Golf Digest* Magazine

INTRODUCTION BY *Cary Middlecoff*

Coward-McCann, Inc. New York

Contents

Introduction

ON the eve of a Masters
Tournament back in one of those years of fond mem-
ory, when the state of my golf game was of some inter-
est to the public, a sportswriter asked me what I
thought of my chances in the upcoming competition.

I replied that I was hitting the ball most satisfactorily
from tee to green, but that unless my putting improved
miraculously—overnight—I couldn't envision myself in
front of the clubhouse late Sunday afternoon accepting
the bright green jacket traditionally presented to the
new Masters champion.

"What seems to be wrong with your putting?" the
writer asked.

At first the question struck me as absurd, and I
started to answer that if I knew what was wrong I
would be out on the putting green trying to correct

it. Then I realized that what the man was asking made sense—that I ought at least to be trying to find out why I couldn't seem to hole a putt.

So I said, "I wish I knew," picked up my putter and headed for the practice putting green.

Somehow or other—I don't remember exactly how —I did find out what the flaw was, and I putted well enough in the tournament to come in second, just one stroke behind the winner. It was 1959, and the Masters winner that year was a putting genius named Art Wall, who holed five birdie putts on the last six holes.

I was reminded of these events while reading this putting guide by Tom Michael and the editors of *Golf Digest*. As the book says, the history of golf seems always to depend on putting. And as it also demonstrates, you can make yourself a better putter if you approach the problem intelligently and work at it.

The people who have put this book together have done a real and perhaps unique service for golfers everywhere. I think it is superior to other books on the same subject because it encompasses all the successful techniques of putting. Those I had previously read or heard about focused on one golfer describing his own putting style. While this sort of approach probably helped some golfers, it was of no particular value to others.

Golf's Winning Stroke: Putting will be of value to every golfer who reads it. And it will be particularly prized by beginning golfers, because it transfers to the reader the cumulative experience of many successful putters. To assimilate all the putting knowledge contained in this book would be a task well worth the time and effort of every golfer.

If I had to choose the single most valuable section in the book it would be the one on mental attitude. All of us try to think positively about putts, since a positive attitude is undoubtedly the key to good putting. And this section, while not purporting to offer any great psychological "secrets," does point to a logical and workable way to positive thinking on the greens: if you are concentrating on ways to make a putt you can't very well be thinking of ways to miss it—you accentuate the positive and eliminate the negative.

I am also impressed by the advice on not anticipating the possible consequences of a missed putt. This is a fault most common to golfers inexperienced in competition. Experience teaches you that you just can't afford to indulge in this sort of negative thinking.

I note that my theory of approach putting, which calls for thinking in terms of holing the putt instead of trying to get close to the hole, is compared in the book with the widely held theory that the player should picture a three-foot circle around the hole and aim for that. I fully agree with the authors that neither theory is necessarily superior to the other. Different theories work best for different people. Indeed, one of the book's outstanding characteristics is that it is never dogmatic on any one approach to a phase of putting.

As to the mechanics of putting—grip, stance, and so on—it appears to me that the entire subject is covered clearly and concisely, along with the reasoning that lies behind each step. Complete information is here for the reader to put to work to his own best advantage.

Finally, I would like to say something about the authors of the book. I know that the editors of *Golf Digest* know golf; their experience is reflected in the pages of each issue of the magazine they publish. I know it too from having frequently discussed with them the technical aspects of the game.

Tom Michael has been a friend and golf companion of mine ever since I started playing the game more than 35 years ago. I am thoroughly familiar with both his golf game, which is at or near scratch, and with his golf writing style, which appears in two books of mine that he edited—*Advanced Golf*, and *Master Guide to Golf*. I admire him both as a golfer and a golf writer. And his specialty at golf is one-putt greens.

I would not say that this book—or any book—will turn you into a wizard on the greens like Locke, Casper, Palmer, Rosburg, or Barber, to name but a handful of the greats who have outputted me over the past two decades. But I would bet a whole set of clubs that reading this book will make you a better putter than you are right now.

CARY MIDDLECOFF

Memphis, Tennessee
January 30, 1967

GOLF'S WINNING STROKE: *Putting*

1. On Putting

ANYONE who knows anything about the game of golf must agree that *if a golfer improves his putting game it is inevitable that he will become a better golfer simply by reducing the number of strokes he takes on the greens.* Furthermore as you will discover while reading this guide to the art and strategy of putting, other phases of your golf game are definitely affected by your putting game, whether it is for better or worse.

This book prescribes no single, set method for knocking a golf ball into the hole. Putting is much too personal for that. Rather, the book presents, in detail, all the various methods, techniques, and ideas that have proven successful in some degree and thereby gained golfers' acceptance.

The book stresses the more conventional putting

styles, and their many variations, as well as the basic putting fundamentals that all golfers should emphasize, whatever their chosen technique may be.

The cross-handed method, whose most notable exponents are Fred Haas, Jr., and Wes Ellis, Jr., is examined, as is the croquet style, whose adherents include playing pros Bob Duden, Bob Shave, and others, plus thousands of Sunday golfers; also analysed is the split-hand methods used with such conspicuous success by Phil Rodgers, who learned it from Paul Runyan, one of the truly great putters in the history of golf. The Runyan-Rodgers technique calls for placing the right hand well below the left on the shaft—a sort of golfing variation of what is known in baseball as the Cobb-Wagner grip—and using a putter some two or three inches longer than the norm, which is about 35 inches.

Our purpose is not necessarily to cover the whole range of putting techniques solely for the sake of encyclopedic comprehensiveness. Rather, the basic aim is to help the golfer-reader find something that will help his own putting—if only by confirming or disputing some apparently outlandish theory whose validity he questions. As the saying goes, there are a lot of ways to skin a cat, and so it is with putting.

Any book on putting should stress its importance in the overall picture of golf. Examples of putting as a major factor of succesful golf are many:

In winning two National Opens—in 1959 at Winged

Foot in the New York area and at the Olympic Club in San Francisco in 1966—Bill Casper one-putted over 40 percent of the holes. In the 1966 Open, which went 90 holes because it ended in a tie that forced a playoff between Casper and Arnold Palmer, Casper didn't three-putt a green until the ninth hole of the playoff— the eighty-first hole of the tournament. And when asked at San Francisco when he had last putted so well, Casper replied, "At Winged Foot in 1959." The clear inference is that great putting brings victory, provided the rest of the player's game is comparable to that of the other contenders, which Casper's definitely is. If Casper had merely averaged 2 putts per green in these tournaments, he would not even have finished among the first 50 places either at Winged Foot or Olympic.

The above observations, however, merely reflect cold mathematics. They show only that good putting lowered Casper's winning scores by the number of times he one-putted instead of two-putted. But who can doubt that those stroke-saving and nerve-saving one-putt greens kept his confidence and competitive spirit high and thus helped him hit the fine long shots that he needed to reach positions where good putting could make him a winner? No perceptive golfer could doubt that good putting enhanced other areas of Casper's game.

Among others, Gary Player and Cary Middlecoff

have maintained that the confidence so vital to low-scoring golf occurs in a sort of reverse pattern, from green to tee.

In much the same vein, Player has commented frequently on the confidence good putting gives a player. The essence of his theory is that when a bad putter makes an approach shot to the green he seldom makes his best shot because, consciously or unconsciously, he believes it won't make that much difference. He doesn't believe he can sink a putt, and so lacks the necessary motivation to play his approach shot with enthusiasm and confidence. In short, the difference between the par shooter and the bogey shooter often lies in a wrong attitude toward the approach shot, which in turn comes from poor putting.

Middlecoff spoke recently of the psychological value of being able to lay long approach putts dead to the pin for tap-ins—a knack which, he observed, could be attained only through practice and an adherence to sound putting principles.

"Those longish second putts," Cary said, "take a lot out of you even when you make 'em. When you keep having to make three- and four-foot putts to two-putt a green, it's going to wear you down eventually. You are going to find yourself a shaken and jumpy man as you walk to the next tee."

A classic, and, in some respects, tragic case revealing the futility of trying to win while not putting well is

Ben Hogan's. Nearing his middle fifties, Hogan remains the paragon of shotmakers. Reliable observers who have watched him play for years declare that Hogan simply never makes a really bad shot from tee to green. In fact, he comes closer to the ideal of hitting every green in the regulation number of strokes than any other player. Yet he was never able to win a tournament in which he putted badly, as he invariably did throughout the decade that began around the mid-1950's. Before then, when he putted well, or even just fairly well, he was a consistent winner.

A lockerroom conversation between Jack Burke, Jr., and Hogan, following a round in the 1965 Masters tournament, clearly indicated that both realized the serious effect poor putting was having on Hogan's game. When Hogan said he had carded a 73 on the round, Burke observed that 73 was an excellent score considering the difficulty Hogan was having sinking four-foot putts. Hogan agreed.

As it turned out, Hogan's 73 represented 35 shots to the greens (he hit the par-5 thirteenth in two and all the rest of the holes in regulation) plus 38 putts. This is not to say that Hogan is unaware of the value of good putting or does not work at this phase of the game. He is and does. But somehow the long years of competitive golf seem to have robbed him of the nerve control one needs on the greens.

The Hogan illustration emphasizes that even near-perfection from tee to green will not suffice unless backed up by at least fair putting.

One clear warning should be sounded before we go into details concerning the techniques used by many of golf's great putters. You should not be a conscious, slavish imitator of another golfer's putting style. Such putting masters as Bob Rosburg, Arnold Palmer, and Bill Casper, along with just about every other golfer who has spoken or written on the subject, have counseled specifically against one golfer's trying to make himself a carbon copy of another.

A case in point is Arnold Palmer. Palmer stands to the putt knock-kneed, pigeon-toed, and altogether in what might be described as a hunched-up position. It is clear to the knowledgeable golfer that Palmer evolved his putting stance with a view to eliminating any possible body movement during the stroke. It works for him. But any other golfer might find the Palmer stance merely cramped and uncomfortable.

All putting authorities stress the importance of freedom and comfort in the stance. "Take a comfortable stance" is a piece of advice found in virtually every treatise on putting—usually quite early in the text, and frequently italicized. "Stand just as I do," on the other hand, is conspicuously absent. Yet while you should not try to mimic Palmer's (or anyone else's) stance exactly, you definitely should emulate his efforts to find a putting stance that will provide a feeling of being firmly anchored in place and is free from body movement during the putting stroke. (We shall see later that body movement, or sway, is one of the great enemies of effective putting.)

To carry our warning against excessive imitation further, consider the putting stance of Jack Nicklaus. Its distinctive feature is that Nicklaus' right shoulder is considerably lower than his left. This places the bulk of his weight on his right leg, and gives him the appearance of being sort of hunkered under the ball. Positioning most of one's weight on the right side goes against prevailing putting opinion, which calls for the weight to be either evenly distributed or mostly on the left side. But, as with Palmer, Nicklaus is guarding against the sway, and has found his own best way to do it.

As further illustration that even the most effective methods vary, Bill Casper advises, "Have your weight equally distributed on both feet, or slightly on your left side," while Bob Rosburg counsels, "The weight should be slightly more on the left foot than on the right." This, he claims, seems to make it easier to hit the ball solidly.

Rosburg then goes on to say, "Two of the best putters I know, Jack Nicklaus and Cary Middlecoff, both look as if they are leaning on their right foot when they putt. It may be that it just looks that way because they putt from a crouch. Their weight is probably equally distributed on both feet."

In respects other than stance, the experts differ in theory and practice. The point emphasized here is that the player who aspires to be a better putter should, while adhering to certain fundamentals, develop his own individual style. Let us put it this way:

The object of this book is to create a framework within the limitations of which instinct and natural skill of a player can find its own expression.

2. Mental Attitude

ON the theory that a golfer must give thought to a putt before he starts the physical process that leads to his actually striking the ball, we shall deal with the mental aspects of putting before we take up the mechanics of the stroke.

Various golf authorities have tried to separate, on a percentage basis, the mental and physical components of the game. "Golf is seventy-five percent mental and twenty-five percent physical," says one noted expert. But it is significant that the man who said this has already mastered the physical side of the game (hitting the ball solidly and straight) but still is frequently guilty of mental lapses, such as choosing the wrong club for a crucial shot, playing a risky shot when circumstances clearly indicated a cautious one, thoughtlessly misplaying or misreading a putt.

Probably the relative importance of the mental and physical sides of golf will never be exactly determined, since they are inextricably bound together. It is enough to remember that the mental side is vitally important. You should remember, too, that a good mental attitude is more important in putting than in any other single phase of the game. Sheer weight of numbers alone proves this true. You use your putter many more times in the course of a round than you do any other single club. In a round played strictly according to the book, you would, on a par-72 course, hit 36 shots to the green and take 36 putts (two per green). The driver, which is ordinarily the next most frequently used club, would come into play perhaps 15 times. The more skillful pros, when they shoot a good score, usually take about 30 putts in 18 holes. When they score badly (for them), they take upward of 36 putts. Among these pros —Palmer, Nicklaus, Sanders, Casper—there is a remarkable similarity in the total number of shots it takes them to put the ball on the putting surfaces. When they putt well, they finish at, or near, the top of the field almost as a matter of course. Even among 90-shooters and upward, putts usually comprise more than one-third of the total number of strokes in a given round.

Obviously, if a proper mental attitude is helpful in golf as a whole, it is even more helpful in putting.

Another, and extremely important, fact is that good

putting gives the average golfer the best chance to cut his scores. Long drives and consistently well-struck iron shots may be beyond the physical capabilities of the average golfer, but there is no compelling reason why any normal golfer can't learn to putt as well as a professional, provided he has the time to devote to developing sound putting techniques. Having a positive mental attitude about your ability to do so is a most important starting point.

Probing a bit deeper into the problem, we find that a great many players—particularly the good ones—hit their long shots almost automatically. They know that a well-hit drive is likely to stay in the fairway and finish in at least a fairly good position from which to play the second shot. More often than not it matters little whether the drive winds up in the middle of the fairway or slightly to one side or the other.

Similarly, a full iron shot simply calls for reasonably good execution. It can wind up 40 feet from the hole or right next to the pin; in either case, the shot can rightly be called a good one. Furthermore, most mistakes in judgment or execution between the tee and the green can, in theory at least, be rectified with a good putt.

But once you reach the putting surface, and especially the area within 6 or 8 feet of the hole, the time has come to succeed or fail, to be a hero or a bum. "The buck stops here," as was once said in another context. Hence the greater mental strain that putting places on the golfer and the greater need for a proper mental attitude on the greens.

The significance of the right attitude is far-reaching. It not only prepares you to handle the putting problem at hand—whether sinking a short first putt or getting down in two from a long distance—but also carry that good frame of mind to the next tee and beyond.

Having generally established, then, the imperative need for a correct mental attitude in putting, let us examine its characteristics. Some adjectives that come readily to mind in this connection are "resolute," "self-contained, "alert," "thoughful," "determined," and "confident."

Confidence is perhaps the putter's greatest ally. But it is a psychological fact that you can't assume a truly confident attitude just by wanting to. Confidence is usually built by holing a couple of good putts in the early stages of the round. Most phenomenal rounds begin that way. The history of golf is replete with such examples. To cite just one, Bob Rosburg says of the 1959 PGA Championship, which he won:

"In the last round there at Minneapolis, I holed a twenty-five-foot birdie putt on the second hole and an eighteen-footer on the third. The mental lift propelled me to a sixty-six that won the tournament."

You cannot always simply decide to hole a long putt early in the round to get your confidence going and then do so. But you can definitely help your chances of bringing this about.

The time to begin the mental preparation for putting is the moment your ball gets onto the putting surface. You should then begin to think in terms of making your putt. Note first the general contour of the green as you walk toward it. This can help you judge correctly the direction and degree of break when you actually come to lining up the putt. But more important, observing the green's overall contour starts you off on a constructive train of thought. You begin to think postively. You have the beginning of a "resolute" attitude.

Then, when you start to line up the putt, concentrate on the line the ball must follow to reach the center of the hole. Strive for a mental picture of the ball following the right path and traveling at the speed that will take it into the hole just as it loses its last bit of momentum.

You can train yourself in this sort of thinking. By doing so you can shut out the negative thoughts that rob so many golfers of whatever chance they might have to become good putters. If you are busy figuring out ways to make a putt, you can't be thinking of ways to miss it.

Since you have a choice in this respect—either to think positively or negatively about making the putt—do not start to imagine everything that could possibly go wrong. Don't say to yourself, "I must be careful not to be short and also I must guard against hitting the ball

Mental Attitude [27

too hard." And don't say, "I mustn't underplay the break or overplay it."

Moreover, don't let your mind wander ahead to what the situation will be if you miss the putt. Stick to the business at hand, which is usually making your putt drop.

If, for instance, you hit a particularly nice shot onto the green and have a good chance for a birdie, don't start telling yourself what a shame it would be to fail to capitalize on so great an opportunity.

Similarly, if an opponent holes a long putt, and you find yourself with a short putt for a tie instead of the win you had expected, don't let it throw you.

Neither of the above situations will disturb you, or at least they will be far less likely to, if you just maintain your positive train of thought.

Perhaps the greatest example of positive thinking on the greens is Arnold Palmer's. Palmer exudes confidence and determination from the moment he takes his putter out of the bag onwards. You watch him take off his glove and stick it in his back pocket, hitch up his pants, stare down the line of his putt, and you know that this is a man who means to knock that ball in the hole.

Palmer works almost by inspiration. He seems able to fire himself up by sheer force of will. Not every golfer, of course, is capable of this sort of thinking, which seems at times to amount to a kind of self-hyp-

Arnold Palmer's confidence and determination are evident as he lines up a difficult putt in a major PGA tournament. Arnie's mental attitude on the green has helped him become one of the game's outstanding putters as well as its leading all-time money-winner.

nosis. But every golfer can at least, if he works at it, think positively enough to convince himself that he will hit the putt to the best of his ability and give himself a good chance to succeed. Just by training yourself to think affirmatively, you can markedly improve your putting.

Many ordinary golfers marvel at the pros' ability to make putts when large sums of money and important championship titles are at stake. "I'd freeze so tight I couldn't even get the putter back" is the typical comment when a Nicklaus or a Casper or a Palmer holes a vital putt in the late stages of an important tournament. And, indeed, putting under such pressure is not an easy thing. But it is much easier if the man with the putter has trained himself to think in terms of what it takes to make the putt, instead of the many possible ways it could be missed. All the successful pros have virtually mastered the art of positive thinking on putts, which accounts for their considerable success in minimizing the psychological impact of extreme pressure.

A rather different thinking problem is posed when the putt in question is a long one, and the intention is to two-putt the green, or, to put it negatively, to avoid three-putting.

Long putts, for professional and amateur alike, rank among the most difficult golf shots. The experts have two basic theories about how a golfer should think when faced with a long approach putt. One could be called the "three-foot-circle" theory, the other, the "strive-for-perfection" theory.

A chief exponent of and spokesman for the three-foot-circle theory is Jack Nicklaus, whose many golfing skills include an exceptional ability to lay the ball stone-dead to the cup on long putts. Believing as he does that putting is critically important to success,

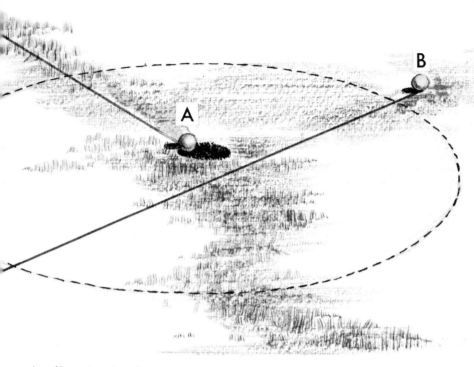

A golfer using the "three-foot circle" theory for long putts imagines
a circle with a three-foot radius around the hole. He is confident that
he can play his first putt into this large area and certainly avoid
three-putting. This added confidence increases his chances of actually sinking his initial putt (A). If he does not finish inside the circle
(B), his second putt is a tough one.

Nicklaus has often emphasized the particular need to
have a strategy for the long putts. The three-foot-circle
method he recommends is intended to prevent three-
putt greens. It is a defensive tactic. It consists, simply,
of imagining a circle, six feet in diameter, surrounding
the hole, then putting to make the ball come to rest
within the circle. Allowing for a margin of error of

the full diameter of the circle (six feet), Nicklaus expects the ball to come to rest within a range of three feet on either side of the cup. With this visual method Nicklaus attempts to avoid the amateur error of long overputts or putts that fall far short of the target.

In contrast to the Nicklaus method, Cary Middlecoff advocates the strive-for-perfection theory:

"My thought is that the proper mental approach to a long putt is, 'I'm going to hole this one by making the ball fall just over the front edge of the cup, just

The "strive-for-perfection" theory is based on the assumption that if you play your first putt to drop the ball right into the hole, you won't leave missed putts very far away.

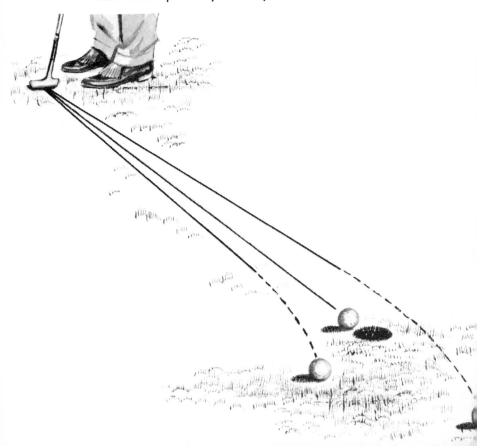

as it loses its last bit of momentum.' In other words, the best way to achieve near-perfection (getting the ball close to the hole) is to strive for perfection (holing the ball)."

"You've probably heard of the magic-circle theory whereby you try to make the ball stop within an imaginary circle with a radius of three feet from the hole. To my mind this is a negative approach to the problem because your goal is near-perfection. Why not try for perfection? It costs no more. If you have in mind that you want to get a long putt within, say, three feet of the cup, you are apt to fall something short of your goal and get it about four feet away. If you picture a perfect putt, it may help you come closer to perfection. And in rare instances you will surprise yourself by achieving perfection. The whole point is that the best way to get close is to try to get in."

The circle theory is based on the assumption that the golfer will be more relaxed and confident if his target is somewhat larger than the cup, whose diameter is four and a quarter inches and which looks mighty small from the edge of a big green.

The Middlecoff strive-for-perfection theory is consistent with his overall thinking about the game, which requires that every shot, including long approach putts, be calculated precisely, and that a mental image of a perfect shot be formed before starting the stroke.

The logical thing to do, of course, is to try both

theories of long putting—"strive for perfection" and "magic circle"—and adopt the one that best suits you.

Two more adjectives describing a proper mental attitude on the greens are "alert" and "thoughtful." As we indicated earlier, you should stay sufficiently alert that you concentrate on succeeding on the putt, entirely excluding negative thoughts about the possibilities or consequences of failure.

Also, you should stay alert in order to learn what you can from putts by other players. If another player's putt is in somewhat the same style as yours, and he must putt before you do, you will naturally want to observe what his ball does on its route toward the cup. Such observation will add to your knowledge of the speed and break (if any) of the portion of the green you will be putting over. What you see may make you want to alter your own putting plan. Or it may confirm your own earlier judgment of the situation. In either case you will be helped.

You can also learn from putts that differ from the one you have coming up. One or two examples should make this point clear. Let's say that you have a 20-foot putt from above the cup. Another player in your group has a 25-foot putt from below the cup. His putt seems headed for the cup, but breaks sharply left as it nears the hole and misses. This missed putt should suggest to you the possibility that your putt, coming from the opposite direction, may take more of a right break at the cup than you had supposed. You should probably take another look at the area near the cup.

In a perhaps more practical vein, let's suppose that your putt runs two or three feet past the hole. Now you will be putting back along the same line as the putt that you saw break sharply left at the hole. Will your own shorter putt do the same? You don't automatically assume that it will. But you do bear it in mind. And you do take a closer look.

In short, keep your eyes open and try to learn from what you see—as the experts do. All you must guard against is letting your eyes deceive you. Suppose, for example, that a player putting before you and in your general style leaves his ball several feet short. Does that mean the green is slower than you had thought? Or slower than it looks? Not necessarily. Perhaps the first player misread the green and simply hit the ball with too soft a stroke. Or perhaps he struck the ball off center and consequently lost power. Be alert to the different factors involved.

Alertness and thoughtfulness on the greens are indispensable adjuncts of sound putting strategy. It must be understood that the really good putter is a sound strategist. He stays alert to what is going on and tries to profit from it. He thinks out situations and tries to turn them to his advantage.

Most strategic situations in putting, as they relate to the other player or players in your group, arise in

Very often you will find that you can "go to school" by watching the break on your partner's or opponents' putt. Even if your putt is from the opposite direction, you might encounter the same slope of the green.

match play. Some are obvious: if you need two putts to win the hole, you clearly want to incorporate a measure of safety in your first putt, to make it essentially a lag. If one putt is needed to tie the hole, you need give no thought to where the ball might end up if you miss. In the first instance, you should think in terms of both the first putt and the second. In the latter instance, you think only in terms of holing your first putt. These strategic situations are, of course, elementary. With two putts to win, it would be ridiculous to bang away at the hole with no thought of the need for making the second putt as easy as possible. It would be equally pointless to use two-putt psychology when one putt is needed to tie.

Even in these situations, true putting strategy goes deeper than it might appear. With two putts to win, you must guard mentally against being too cautious. Don't feel that you must leave the ball short of the hole just because you are trying to lag it up close. A putt that runs six inches past the hole is also a good lag. If you focus too intently on not going by the hole, you may hit the ball so short that you leave yourself a tough second putt.

It is vitally important in this two-putts-to-win situation that you not let yourself be lulled into a false sense of security. Do not assume that the hole is over for all practical purposes, and that any sort of half-hearted effort on your part will finish the job. Keep thinking (stay alert), for two big reasons. One is that if you hit that first putt lackadaisically, you may end up three-putting and tying the hole. Second, you don't stand to have two putts to win very often. If you muff so excellent a chance, you will probably be discouraged about the holes ahead and, at the same time, give your opposition a valuable mental lift. What you do in this sort of situation can easily be the key to winning or losing the match. Don't take it lightly.

In the one-putt-to-tie situation, a danger is giving too much thought to getting the ball at least up to the hole. The point is to get the ball in the hole, not past it. Paul Runyan, a master putter, takes exception to the attitude of the player who believes that 10 feet beyond the hole on a 20-foot putt is somehow better than falling short of the hole. Runyan contends that the "at-least-I-gave-it-a-chance" attitude is a very bad putting habit.

The same reasoning applies when you have a "free" putt in partnership play. Say your partner has already made a 5 and you have a putt of reasonable length for a 4. If you bang it at the hole largely to be able to say, "I had to get it there," you need to revise your thinking. Similarly, if you leave this sort of putt a turn short, and your partner criticizes you for not "going for it," his is the faulty thinking. The putt that falls a few inches short indicates you have made a good sensitive effort. Certainly a putt that goes far beyond the hole is as poor a putt, poorly conceived and poorly executed, as one that falls far short.

Partnership play offers numerous chances to exercise winning strategy on the greens. If it is your turn to putt, you may elect to have your partner, who is closer to the hole, putt before you do. If your partner's shorter putt is similar to yours, and he has taken more strokes up to that point than you have, you could ask him to putt first in order to give you a better idea of the speed and break of the green. Or if your partner has a short putt for, say, a 5, and you are putting for a 4, you might ask him to try his putt first to cinch a 5 for your side. If he makes his 5, you will, of course, be relieved about a second putt in case you miss your first try. If he misses his putt, you will at least be certain of what you have to do.

Two rather subtle factors enter into the strategy of handling the situations described above. Some players, by reason of temperament, would rather not have their partner putt out first, preferring to keep the comfortable knowledge that partner is up close and that the partnership will have two short putts for a 5 in case your putt for a 4 does not succeed. Second, some players do not like to putt out ahead of their partner. They feel they can putt better if they actually know whether or not the putt is important. Usually the decision should be made by the player with the longer putt.

Sometimes partners will have putts of approximately

LIES 3

LIES 4

When you are playing with a partner in four-ball competition, strategy on the green becomes extremely important. Above, Partner A lies three and is about 17 feet from the cup on this par-5 hole. Partner B lies four and is 3 feet from the pin. Partner B will sink his easy putt first to insure the par for the team. This will allow Partner A to putt boldly for a team "birdie" with the knowledge that even if he misses badly it cannot hurt the team because of Partner B's par.

equal length for the same score. In such cases, the weaker player in the partnership might want to putt first, even though his putt is slightly shorter. This would allow the weaker player to putt under less intense pressure.

In stroke play, the strategic question of caution versus boldness seldom comes into clear focus until late in the round. If you have a good lead with only a few holes left to play, you should begin to minimize your risks. Or if you are trailing with only a few holes left, logic may call for bolder play. In neither case, however, should you go to great extremes of caution or boldness. Many a stroke-play tournament has been lost because the leader began too soon to resort to arch-conservatism. At the opposite extreme, many have been lost because a contender began to take foolish risks when good, steady play would have brought him home in front.

In all kinds of golf competition there are times for caution and times for boldness. But intelligent play, on the greens and elsewhere, is always required. The great players, the ones who make the winning putts, have remarkably similar theories concerning the right mental attitude for putting. In essence, they come to this:

Think positively and trust your own best judgment and your putting stroke.

Many golfers, including some of the best professionals, consider and follow the advice of their caddy (if he has proved to be a good caddy with a knowledge of the course) about the speed and break of the greens. Also, many golfers like to seek a partner's opinion about how a given putt should be played. (Under the rules, your caddy and your partner are the only ones from whom you can get advice.) In this connection, remember these two major points:

1. If you are asking advice about how much a given putt will break, or whether it will break at all, your caddy or partner cannot be sure of how firmly or softly you are going to hit the putt. A firmly struck putt, for example, will break less than one that is hit just hard enough to reach the front of the hole. "Play a three-inch left break," your adviser might say, and then you hit a firm putt that breaks left only half that much, when the same putt, hit just hard enough to reach the hole, would have broken the full three inches. The reverse, of course, can also be true; your adviser may be thinking of a firmly struck putt, and you hit a "dying ball" putt that breaks off below the hole. Many expert putters rely on outside advice only for the direction, not the degree of break. (The relationship of break to speed will be more fully discussed in the following chapter.)

2. Advice can confuse almost as easily as help you. If it confirms your own thinking, you will have a more positive attitude and probably will hit the putt more

confidently. But if it contradicts your thinking, you almost certainly will have trouble deciding how to play the putt. The resulting stroke is likely to be hesitant, doubtful, and ineffective.

If you do seek advice, it is usually best to preface your question with a description of your own estimate of the situation. For instance, "I think I should hit this putt firmly and play about a two-inch left break. Is that about the way you see it?" This sort of question gives your adviser more to go on. The wise adviser won't be likely to contradict you unless he is convinced you have sized the putt up incorrectly.

Actually, whether advice will help or hurt you depends upon your own temperament. Some players are undoubtedly helped and they habitually seek such help. Others feel advice can only confuse and never seek it. A third group may or may not seek advice, depending on whether they think the particular putt calls for an outside opinion. The wisest golfers are probably found in the third group.

Part of the mental approach to putting involves the "dying-ball" theory versus the "hit-it-in-the-back-of-the-cup" theory. Many great putters, among them the immortal Robert T. Jones, Jr., held firm to the dying-ball theory, which calls for trying to hit the putt just hard enough to reach the hole, thus giving the ball a chance to fall in from the front or either side of the cup or even curl around and fall in from the back.

The theory that a dying ball gives you four ways to enter the cup—front, back, left and right sides—has been advanced by many noted players such as Bobby Jones. They contrast the advantage of this strategy with the disadvantage of the firmly hit putt aimed at the back of the cup, which has only one possible entrance: the front of the cup.

The hit-it-in-the-back-of-the-cup theorists contend that a firmly hit putt will hold its line better and not veer off as it nears the hole. The old "never up, never in" bromide is a favorite with this group. No doubt it is true that a firmly hit putt does hold its line better. Arnold Palmer, for example, whose success as a putter is a matter of record, is one who tends to go boldly for the back of the cup. Yet we must remember that Palmer's entire personality is far from conservative. Charging putts suit his confident manner. He is also one of the game's outstanding "comeback" putters.

A point that should always be considered in planning the speed of a putt is that the diameter of the hole (4.25 inches) is more than twice the diameter of the ball (1.68 inches). Therefore, if your putt travels at the right speed and is generally on target, you have a sizable margin for error and are still able to sink the putt.

Theories aside, the great putters—even Bobby Jones in his heyday—bang in some putts, trickle in others, and hit still others at what might be called medium speed. They don't rigorously follow either of the theo-

The relationship between the diameter of the hole and that of your golf ball definitely allows a wide margin of error on all putts. Actually the hole is more than two times wider than your golf ball.

ries described above. Rather, they use the best features of both to advantage. And so should you.

"In putting," said Paul Runyan, "you are confronted by two truths difficult to reconcile. If you don't get the ball up it can't go in. But for each added bit of speed it has less of the hole to hit."

One more adjective describes an important aspect of the proper mental attitude in putting. The word is "decisive." It is crucial to make a firm decision on how you mean to play a putt—and then to stick to it.

Many of your decisions will, of course, be wrong. Even the greatest putters sometimes miscalculate the speed or break, or both, of a particular putt. The average player naturally makes even more mistakes. No golfer has ever lived who hasn't said, or at least thought, "I hit the putt exactly the way I wanted to, and still missed it." But more often than not, your estimate of the putting situation will be basically correct.

The point is that you cannot logically expect to make a putt if you are uncertain when you stroke the ball. Cloudy thinking will be directly reflected in a hesitant, jerky putting stroke. If you find yourself standing over a putt with your mind assailed by doubts, step away from the ball and make a clear decision before proceeding.

Correct mental attitude becomes especially important on those little putts of two feet or less—the kind which should be successful every time, but which occasionally are missed even by the best players. Most are missed through carelessness, some because the player becomes so hypercautious that he tenses up completely and manages to overcomplicate what is essentially a simple operation.

The idea, then, is to exercise reasonable care on these little putts but not to overdo it. Simply look at the line, set yourself properly and give the ball your best stroke.

For those who generally compete at match play, which includes nearly all golfers except the touring pros, the subject of very short putts includes the problem of when to concede an opponent a putt, and when to expect him to concede one to you. Technically speaking, conceding putts has no real place in the game of golf, and, obviously, the subject is not covered in the rules. For practical purposes, however, these so-called "gimmie" putts do enter into the overall strategy of golf.

Walter Hagen, renowned as a great golf psychologist as well as great player, would concede his opponents a few "missable" puts early in the match. Then, in the later stages, he would introduce the element of surprise by making his opponents hole putts even shorter than the ones he had been conceding. In his amateur days when he was competing mainly in match play tournaments, Jack Nicklaus had a theory that a strategic advantage might sometimes be gained by making the opponent putt even the shortest putts on the first few holes, then conceding the very short ones in the middle stage of the match, then reverting to the "no-gimmie" tactic on the final holes. He reasoned that the opponent might well be a little shaky at the start and might therefore miss a short one. Later, when his opponent had become accustomed to expecting concessions, Nicklaus tried to shake him up a little by not giving anything.

The best way to handle this situation, according to

a number of experts, is never to concede a putt when you think there is even the slightest chance of a miss, and never to expect even the shortest putt to be conceded to you. You are under no obligation to concede any putt even though your opponent may be conceding putts to you. It isn't a matter of sportsmanship, but rather of common sense.

Proper mental attitude for putting carries beyond the striking of the last putt on a given green. Consideration should also be given to how to react when you miss a short putt, or two or three in a row, that you ought to have made. There are two basic ways a golfer can react to missed short putts. One is with anger, frustration, and a feeling that fate has singled him out as its patsy. This is obviously the wrong reaction, wrong because if you indulge yourself in it, you are setting yourself up for more missed putts and a rotten golf game in general.

The other way is to accept a missed short putt as something that is bound to happen to everyone at one time or another, and to analyze the cause of the error in order to prevent its recurrence. If you train yourself to react in this positive manner, you will be on your way to maturity and greater excellence as a golfer. Remember that if you lose your poise over a missed short putt, you are not only hurting your own game, you are also giving aid and comfort to the opposition.

3. Physical Aspects

It is a rare thing to accomplish a putt of more than 5 or 6 feet that will follow an absolutely straight line to the hole. Nearly all greens are contoured to some degree, which means that virtually every sizable putt will veer in one direction or the other along its route to the hole. Besides the breaks (slopes) in the green, you also usually have the problem of "grain"— the direction in which the blades of grass are growing.

Judging the correct path along which to try to send the ball into the hole is called "reading the green." This involves both slope and grain. First consider the matter of slope (or contour, or slant).

Survey the general slope of a green as you walk toward the putting surface. You will get a better perspective of the contours from somewhat of a distance, say 50 yards away, than you will when you are actually on the green.

If, for instance, you are studying the line of a putt and you simply cannot be certain whether there is a break or not, call on the knowledge you gained from surveying the green as you approached it. Did the green as a whole seem to slope slightly toward you? Or away from you? Or to one side or the other? Or did it appear quite level? The answer would provide a clue as to whether to play for a break on your putt.

The same knowledge, of course, can help settle questions in your mind about the degree of break to play. But it should be emphasized that the main advantage of this preliminary study of the green from afar is to resolve less obvious putting lines. Actually, you can usually pick out the right path for a putt simply by looking along the line from behind the ball.

This brings up the question of whether you should line up a putt by looking from cup to ball as well as from ball to cup. Bob Rosburg, for one, advises against this double look: "I can see the line when kneeling down in back of the ball, looking toward the hole, better than in any other way," says Rosburg. "Sometimes I walk halfway toward the hole and look from the side. This gives me a better impression of the distance and the degree of sidehill terrain."

Other experts warn against the double look on the grounds that it tends to confuse the player. If a putt's line looks different from hole to ball than it does from ball to hole, you may not know which impression is most reliable. If it looks the same, the second look is largely a waste of time, your time as well as that of your playing companions, plus that of any player directly behind you on the course. Many experts also agree that your first impression is usually the best.

One fact must be understood in judging breaks: the amount of break a putt will take is in inverse ratio to the speed at which the ball will be traveling. A downhill putt tapped gently and rolling slowly will take more break than a more firmly stroked uphill putt of equal length over comparable terrain.

"If the ball is traveling quite slowly," says Cary Middlecoff, "it will follow whatever break there is in the green. On the other hand, if it's moving briskly, its momentum will keep it more on line."

Middlecoff, recognized as one of the great theorists of the game and for a decade one of its greatest practitioners, goes on to say:

"The problem of force versus break arises when you're not certain whether the ball will take a slight break or travel along a straight line to the hole. If you decide to play the break, use only enough force to carry the ball over the front lip of the cup. Then if there is a slight break, the ball will take it. Conversely, if you decide to play the putt straight at the hole, you should hit it rather firmly. In that way, it will hold its line against a slight break that's not obvious."

The importance of putting the short ones (up to 3

feet) as though there were no break was often stressed by Tommy Armour. He meant that on these short putts you should bang the ball at the back of the cup hard enough for its momentum to keep it on line. But Armour seems to be in the minority on this point. Certainly it would take a very bold man to putt this way on all short putts, especially on a downhill-sidehill putt on a fast green.

The rate of speed of a putt will determine how much the ball will break on its path to the hole. A putt moving fast (right) will break less than normal (left). A very slow putt (center) will break much more severely than normal.

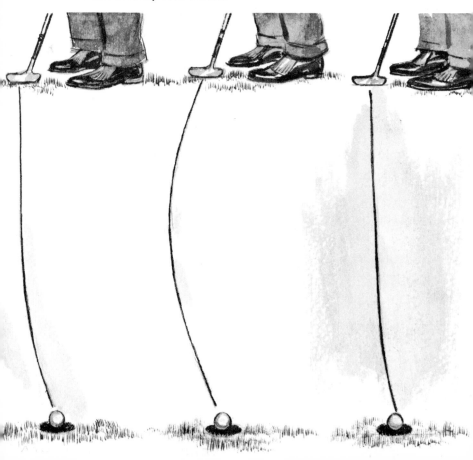

Middlecoff makes some further comments on breaking putts:

"The greater the distance a ball rolls along a slanted green, the more it will veer in the direction of the slant. But we cannot assume that the ball will roll at the same speed all the way along the slant and that it will break twice as far on a twenty-four-foot putt as it will on a twelve-foot putt. Because the ball does not maintain a constant speed on a putt, the break isn't consistent throughout. In the early stages of the putt, the ball will be traveling with greater force and hence will tend to stay more on line. The sharper break starts when the ball nears the hole and begins to roll more slowly.

"The green may show a sharp break for the first few feet along which a putt will travel, and then level out as the ball nears the hole. Under such conditions, the tendency is to attach too much importance to the early break. The player allows for too much overall break and leaves the ball on the high side of the cup. The proper approach is to minimize the early break because the ball will have greater momentum in the early stages and will hold more closely to a straight line. Conversely, when the sharper slope is near the hole, allow for maximum break."

This explains why good putters closely examine the area within a 3- or 4-foot radius of the hole. They know that this is where the ball will be most affected by any break that is present.

In recent years a technique for determining green slant, called the "plumb-line method," has come into vogue. It is generally described this way:

Stand directly behind the ball, lining it up with the hole. Suspend the putter in front of you so that it hangs free, straight down. Sighting with only one eye open, cover (hide) the ball with the lower part of the putter shaft. Then, without moving either the putter or your head, look up at the hole. If the hole shows to the right of the shaft, the putt will break to the right, by the amount indicated. It will break left if the hole shows to the left of the shaft. If the top of the shaft "covers" the hole, the putt is straight.

This method is recommended mainly for use on courses in the mountains or by the sea. On mountain courses in particular, optical illusions can play tricks. The green may seem perfectly level when you are standing on it, but actually it will nearly always be sloping away from the nearest mountain. Similarly, greens on seaside courses nearly always slope toward the sea, although the slope may be imperceptible. In these situations, the plumb-line method of surveying the situation can be most helpful.

Most plumb-line advocates say you should sight with your master eye, which raises the question of which one that is. If you are right-handed, chances are your right

Plumb-line sighting will tell you which way the ball will roll. By aligning the shaft of the putter over the ball and sighting with your dominant eye, you can expose the direction the ball must be played to break toward the hole.

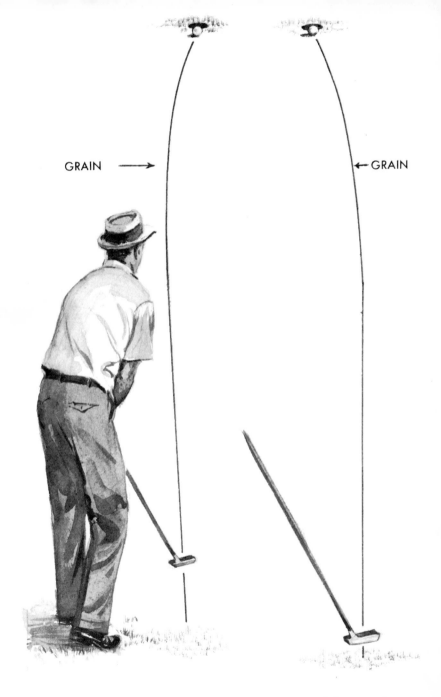

GRAIN →   ← GRAIN

A putt will always break in the direction the grain of the grass is running. If the grain is running to the right, the putt will break to the right. The reverse is true when the grain is running to the left.

eye is your master eye; if left-handed, your left eye dominates. But there are exceptions to this rule. You can settle the question by a simple test. Select an object some 15 feet away that is about the size of your fist. A golf hole will do nicely if you happen to be making the test at a course. With both eyes open, point at the object with your right index finger. Then close one eye. If you seem still to be pointing directly at the object, it is your master eye that is open. If you close your master eye and open the other, it will appear that the object has moved a few inches to one side.

The other important element in determining whether the ball will follow a straight or curved line to the cup is grain, which, as noted earlier, refers to the direction in which the blades of grass on the green are growing. If you are putting across the grain, the ball will, to some degree, curve in the direction in which the grain runs. The degree depends, naturally, on the length of the putt, the speed of the ball, and the thickness and length of the grass.

The ability to "read the grain" is specifically of value in determining how hard a given putt must be hit in order to reach the hole. Putting against the grain is like putting uphill; putting with the grain, like putting downhill. However, grain is more difficult to detect, more subtle, than the slant of a green. The difference in putting with or against the grain of a green is comparable to planing a piece of wood with or against the grain. The principle is the same.

Grain is established in a number of ways, either singly or in combination. The movement of water draining across a green can determine grain. So can a prevailing wind. With Bermuda grass, particularly, grain will occur if the green is regularly mowed in the same pattern. Bermuda-grass greens, incidentally, are more grainy than bent-grass greens. They are common in the southern part of the United States or wherever the summer climate is hot and moist, since Bermuda grass can thrive only in warm weather. Rye grass, which survives only in cool or cold weather, is usually substituted for Bermuda in the winter. Bent is a year-round grass grown principally in the northern half of the United States and along the East and West Coasts.

Whatever the type of grass, the prescribed test for determining grain is basically the same: look for "shine." Stand behind your ball and look along the surface of the grass in the direction of the cup. If the surface presents a shiny, or glazed, appearance, you will be putting with the grain. If there is no shine, if the surface appears dull, you will be putting against the grain.

On sidehill putts, you will frequently encounter situations in which both slope and grain are factors. The grain may offset, or partially offset, the break that the slope alone would give the putt. Or the grain may ac-

GRAIN

GRAIN

If the grain of the grass is running toward you, the ball will travel slower (left) than if the grain is running toward the hole (right).

centuate the break caused by the slope. This is why it is essential to know as much as possible about reading greens.

Once you have determined the amount of break that a given putt will take—or think you have—the next question is how to line yourself up to allow for the break.

One technique used by many golfers, but recommended by virtually no experts, is to line up with the hole as if the putt were straight, and then try to push or pull the putt by the amount indicated by the probable break.

Another and better method is mentally to move the cup to the left or right as indicated by the break, and then line up with the imaginary cup instead of the real one. The late Horton Smith, in his prime considered the paragon of putters, used and recommended this method. Other experts favor it for short putts only.

A third way of handling the problem is called "spot putting." You sight along the curving line that you think the ball should follow and find something that catches the eye—a spot of grass of a different color from the rest, perhaps, or the filled-in place where a previous cup had been cut. Then you line up with that spot.

Your spot need not, of course, be directly on the intended line of your putt. It can be to one side or the other. In that case, you say to yourself that the ball

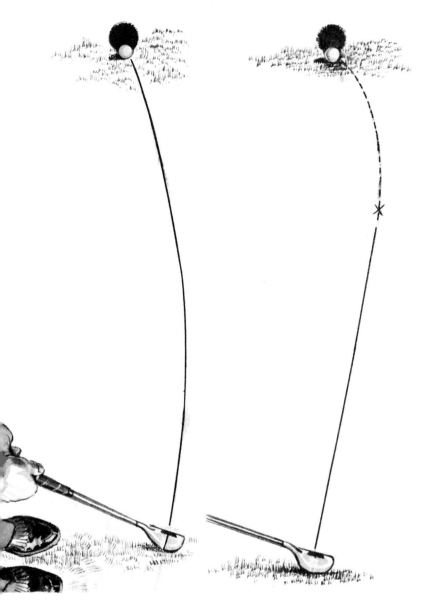

The two most popular methods used for playing putting breaks are (1) at left, to envision an imaginary "break line" from your lie to the hole and play your ball directly in, and (2) at right, to pick a spot either to the right or left of the cup which you feel indicates the peak of the break and putt to this spot, letting the break do the rest of the work of getting the ball to the hole.

must go just above (or just below) the spot you have picked and line up accordingly.

Sam Snead, whose tremendous ability as a long putter has been obscured by his reputation for missing some important short putts, is a great exponent of the spot method. Quite often he uses two (or sometimes three) spots along his intended line. As he stands over the ball and looks along his line, his eyes will pause noticeably at the first spot, then pick up the line again and follow it to his next marker.

Some fine players combine the spot-putting method with the technique of mentally moving the cup, using the former on long putts and the latter on short ones.

Others find an examination of the hole itself useful in determining green slant. If one side of the hole appears slightly higher than the other, you may be reasonably sure that the green slants in the direction of the lower side, and that the ball will break that way as it nears the hole. This is a good test to try after you have applied the more obvious ones and are still in doubt about the break.

Another factor that must be taken into account is the texture (height and thickness) of the grass. If the green's texture is such that the ball will be rolling more through the grass than over it, as will be the case if the grass is fairly high and lush, you should play for a minimum break. The same holds true on a wet green.

There are two elements in this theory. One is that

the higher grass (or water) on the low side will resist the break of the ball in that direction. The other is that a putt over a slow green must naturally be hit harder, and its extra momentum in the early stages will keep the break to a minimum.

If the green is hard and closely clipped, the ball will roll along the top of the grass, and you should allow for the maximum break that you see. As we have noted, a slowly rolling ball will take the full break. Also, there

When a green is freshly cropped, your ball will travel much faster (top) than it will on a green that has not been cropped for several days. Look carefully at the height of the blades of grass before getting ready to putt.

FAST GREEN

SLOW GREEN

will be no resistance to the ball's breaking to the lower side.

With reference to breaking putts, you probably have heard the expressions "pro side" and "amateur side." A player who misses a putt through playing for too much break may say, "Well, I kept it on the pro side." Putts that miss on the lower side of the cup are said to have been missed on the "amateur side." This distinction has some slight merit. As long as the ball is on the high side of the cup, there is at least a theoretical chance that it may topple in, but all chance is lost once the ball breaks below the cup.

Experts use this technique mainly on approach putts, in situations where the principal objective is to get the ball near the cup for a tap-in. As long as the ball is rolling toward the high side of the hole, the slant of the green is helping to slow the ball down. Once the ball breaks below the hole, there is no slant to resist its trickling on down the slope and away from the hole.

Wind can affect the roll of a putt. All of us probably have seen a putt roll up to the very lip of the cup and hang there tantalizingly with part of the ball over the edge of the hole. Whether or not it finally drops may depend on the wind. A following wind may give it the tiny bit of force necessary. An adverse wind can hold it in place and keep it from dropping. Wind does have an effect, even on a ball rolling along the ground. This is particularly important when the green is hard and fast, when the ball must roll along on top of the grass rather than, to some degree, through the grass.

When should you take the wind into account in judging the break of a putt? The correct answer probably should be, "Almost never." Rare exceptions can occur when the wind is very strong and the green very fast. In the few instances where wind should be considered a factor, you must use your own best judgment. No clear rules can be laid down for such a subtle and infrequent calculation.

A word of caution about "overreading" the greens is in order. As noted earlier in this chapter with respect to scanning at the line of a putt, both from ball to hole and hole to ball, some things can be at once a source of confusion and a waste of time.

Certainly you wouldn't want to apply every test and technique we have mentioned to all your putts. To do so would defeat your primary purpose—making the putt. By the time you have lined up the putt from every angle, applied the plumb-line test and several others, you will be so distracted that you will have no chance at all to stroke the putt properly.

Another disadvantage of trying to apply all the tests is that you will take up so much time that your playing partners will abandon you on the first green, suggesting that you go on with your survey while they play golf.

Do only what is necessary to get a generally clear

idea of the line of your putt. If it is a simple putt, deal with it simply and briskly. If it is a tricky putt, take a little extra time to study the situation. But deal only with the essentials. Don't go out of your way to add complications.

As Bill Casper says:

"Don't get the reputation as a 'surveyor' of the greens. Too many golfers go through a ritual of surveying every blade of grass on the green before putting. Establish an orderly procedure of studying putts, starting from the time you walk onto the green to the actual execution of the stroke. After a little practice, you will be surprised how quickly you can master a putting procedure that will not waste your time or that of your playing partners."

4. The Grip

IF you were to spend a day around the practice putting green during one of the major golf tournaments—for instance, the Masters or the National Open—you would see what at first might appear to you as a bewildering variety of ways to grip a putter. This would be true even if you confined your observations to those players with conventional putting styles, and did not take into account the rare ones who putt cross-handed, or croquet fashion, or with the hands separated on the club by several inches.

On closer examination, you would see that the putting grips of virtually all the leading players have one main thing in common. And if you had the opportunity to hear each one describe the basics of his putting grip, you would note a remarkable similarity of opinion on this common point:

"In developing a proper grip you should strive to position your hands so that the palms oppose, or face, each other on the putter shaft.... With the palms opposed ... the putter blade can be kept square to the line much more easily." (Bill Casper)

"The back of the left hand faces the line of the putt." (Bob Rosburg)

Arnold Palmer favors having the back of his left hand facing the hole, with palms facing each other. Dow Finsterwald recommends keeping the hands in similar juxtaposition. Ken Venturi strives to strike the ball with the blade square by keeping the back of his left hand and the palm of his right facing the hole. Raymond Floyd, another expert, also favors palms in opposition.

And so on down the line, with an occasional exception that amounts more to a personal modification than a different concept. For instance, Jerry Barber keeps the back of his left hand facing the hole, while his right hand is turned just a bit more under the shaft than is the case with those mentioned above.

Great golfers of the past also confirm this principle. The late Horton Smith came out four-square for having the back of the left hand facing the intended line directly, with the palms exactly opposing each other. Paul Runyan, another of the greats of a slightly earlier era, said that the hands should directly oppose each other, although, like Barber, he added a modification

Most golfers use a putting grip which has the palm of the right hand and the back of the left hand facing down the putting line throughout the stroke (left). Although Jerry Barber keeps the back of his left hand facing the target, he rotates his right hand slightly behind the shaft (below). He feels that this gives him more control on his stroke.

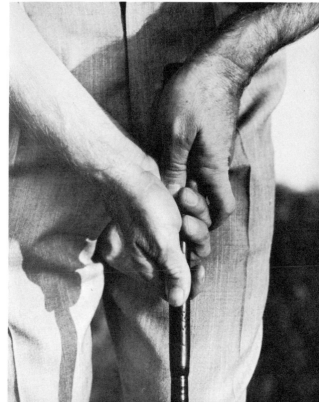

of his own. Runyan set the left hand and the right hand farther under the shaft than would be considered standard, but held to the theory of the hands opposing each other.

Out of the more distant past, and from England, Joyce Wethered, whom many regard as the greatest woman player in the history of golf, theorized similarly: "Keep the back of the left hand facing toward the hole rather than showing on top of the shaft and the back of the right hand at the same time well behind the shaft."

The same reasoning underlies the precepts laid down by Robert T. "Bobby" Jones, Jr., who, in addition to being one of the greatest golfers of all time, was also one of the most articulate.

Jones emphasized a grip with the thumbs on top of the shaft, the back of the left hand and the palm of the right facing the hole. This positioning is intended to avoid twisting the club face out of alignment with line of the putt.

Like Jones, virtually all distinguished authorities on putting stress placing the thumbs straight down the top of the shaft. But this thumb placement is more a corollary to having the hands oppose each other than a separate feature of the putting grip. With the back of the left hand and the palm of the right hand facing directly along the intended line, the natural position for the thumbs will be straight down the top of the shaft.

A number of great putters stress the role that the thumbs—the right thumb, in particular—play in the putting stroke. Bobby Jones theorized that pressing only the tip-end joint of the right thumb, not its whole length, to the club provided a sensitive touch that results in accurate putting control. A few experts like Johnny Farrell went even further, exerting pressure on the club only with the end of the thumb. Farrell also pressed his thumbnail into the grip.

This stress on thumb placement assumes greater significance when illustrated by what might be called "the George Low story." Low played in some professional tournaments with indifferent success back in the 1930's and '40's. Several years ago he virtually abandoned all phases of golf except putting, at which he is an acknowledged wizard. He claims he can beat anybody in the world in putting, and is rarely challenged to prove it. A number of leading professionals, recently including Jack Nicklaus, have taken putting lessons from him.

Low makes something of a mystery out of his uncanny ability to putt, but he has said on several occasions that the key is in the thumbs. Low places only the first joint of both the right and left thumbs on top of the shaft and presses downward with them, with a light but clearly defined pressure.

All of which lends credence to the theory that thumb

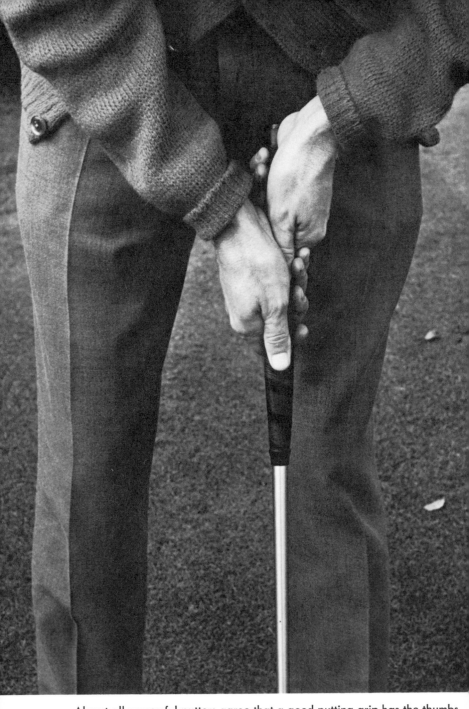

Almost all successful putters agree that a good putting grip has the thumbs of both hands going straight down the top of the shaft. This minimizes the possibility of turning the club at any point during the stroke.

The position of and the pressure generated by the right thumb is extremely important to the "feel" of your putting grip. Some leading golfers believe that the tip of the right thumb should be off the shaft with the pressure in the ball of the finger (above). Some putters, including the great Bobby Jones, advocate pressing only the tip of this thumb into the club's grip (below).

placement and pressure have a lot to do with developing an effective putting grip. The golfer who aspires to be an outstanding putter, or even just a better putter than he is, would do well to check his own grip with a view to making the adjustments suggested above.

There are endless variations of "proper" putting grips. The most widely used method of placing the hands on the club is called the "reverse overlap" grip. In it the index finger of the left hand overlaps the little finger of the right hand, whereas in the regular overlap grip, the little finger of the right hand overlaps the index finger of the left hand.

Bill Casper, a leading exponent of the reverse overlap method, grips the club with the index finger of the left hand overlapping both the little finger and the third finger of the right hand. He says the basic aim of the putting grip is to develop a sensitive feel with the right hand, which he considers the dominant hand in the putting stroke, while the left hand's main function is to steady the stroke and keep the face of the putter square to the line.

Arnold Palmer's grip is basically the reverse overlap, varying in that the index finger of the left hand is extended straight down to its full length. Many other good putters employ this variation, in the belief that the fully extended left index finger makes a good lever for initiating the backswing.

Bobby Locke uses the regular overlapping grip, usu-

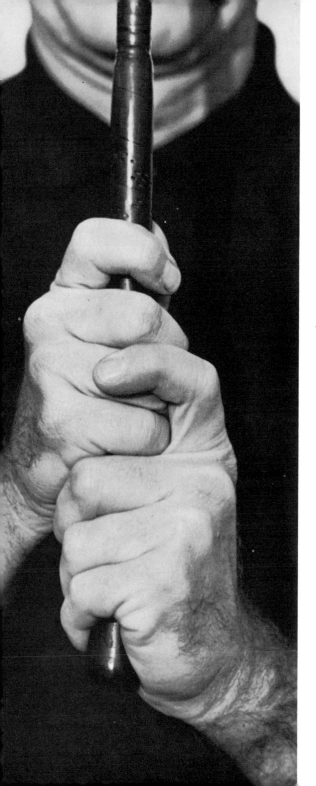

The most commonly used putting grip is the reverse overlap grip in which the forefinger of the left hand overlaps the fourth finger of the right hand.

ally referred to as the Vardon grip, identical to the one he and most other top flight golfers employ for full shots. This also is the putting grip of Johnny Palmer (no relation to Arnold), a onetime Western Open champion and one of the top pros in the years following World War II.

Bob Rosburg and Art Wall, Jr., two of the very best on the greens, use the ten-finger grip (sometimes called the baseball grip) for putting as well as for all their other shots. "I follow the principle of gripping the putter just as I do the rest of my clubs," says Rosburg, "on the theory that this feels most normal." Other experts agree that there is probably an advantage in using the same basic grip for putting as for the other shots, since the putting stroke is essentially a shortened version of the full swing.

Another grip used by a considerable number of golfers but rarely seen among the pros calls for overlapping the little and third fingers of the right hand over the index and middle fingers of the left hand. This grip leaves the left hand in a stronger position than the right, which contradicts the putting theories of most experts.

Several years ago Gene Sarazen began using a grip whose distinguishing feature was that the right index finger was fully extended and positioned along the right side of the shaft. Sarazen called it the "after-40 finger grip." He recommended its use particularly to

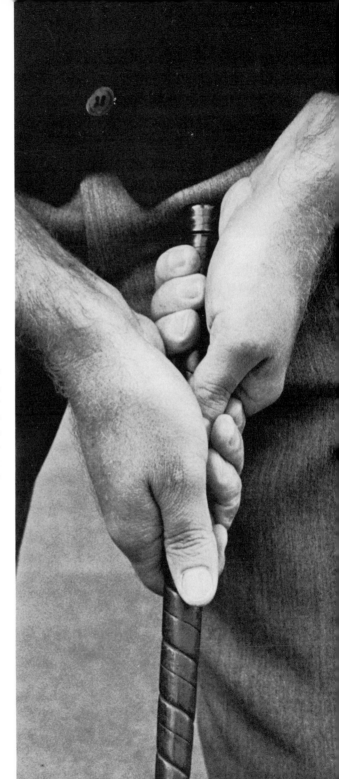

Many leading PGA tour professionals such as Bob Rosburg and Art Wall find that the ten-finger "baseball" grip gives them better control of their putter. In this grip every finger is on the shaft.

older golfers as a better means of steadying the stroke. Many golfers use this grip, although Sarazen himself has not stuck with it consistently.

Perhaps it should be noted here that a number of name golfers over the years have recommended a particular putting grip with which they were having success at the time, then changed to another grip or reverted to an old method shortly afterward. In fact, most golfers continually experiment with various putting methods and gimmicks, discovering that what may work well for a while does not necessarily stand the test of time.

The most curious putting grip presently being used with conspicious success is that of Phil Rodgers, whose name can usually be found high on the list of money winners on the pro tour. Rodgers uses what he calls the "split-grip" technique. He holds the very end of the putter with his left hand tight against his belt, keeping this hand stationary throughout the stroke. His right hand is about a foot below the left, and his grip with the right hand is with the thumb and first three fingers, using a very delicate pressure. The basic purpose of this grip is to achieve a pendulum motion with the putter.

Rodgers was taught the split grip by Paul Runyan. And there may be some significance in the fact that Runyan himself still recommends it highly. At first Runyan found it highly effective on putts of about 15 feet or less, but less so on longer putts. Then he began using a putter with a shaft about 41 inches long, some 6 inches longer than the regular putter shaft length. This longer putter—Rodgers' putter is of similar length —enabled Runyan to produce a controlled stroke even on long putts requiring a more forceful stroke.

The cross-handed putting grip, also called the reverse-handed grip, began to enjoy a considerable vogue about 1965. Fred Haas, Jr., the veteran New Orleans professional who became the United States Seniors champion in 1965, had been using the technique for several years. It was subsequently adopted by such successful pros as Johnny Pott, Wes Ellis, Jr., Jim Ferree, Peter Alliss of Great Britain's Ryder Cup team, and, among the ladies, Marilynn Smith.

As its name implies, the essential feature of this grip is that the hands are crossed, or reversed from their normal position. The right hand is placed on top and the left hand below it by right-handed golfers. There are minor variations of this grip. Ellis describes his own:

"My grip is the interlocking, with the little finger of my left hand twining around the forefinger of my right hand. This is simply a left-handed interlock as might be used by any left-hander. I putt right-handed, however. The back of my left hand and the palm of my right hand face toward the hole. My thumbs are directly on top of the shaft. Both hands feel the same

The Grip [79

Recently some men and women touring professionals adopted a cross-hand putting grip. At right, PGA tour star Johnny Pott demonstrates his techniques.

amount of tension. My hands seem to fit more closely together with the interlock, but I don't think it makes any difference as to the particular kind of grip used so long as it is basically cross-handed. A player simply should experiment until he finds the grip that feels most comfortable for him.

"The thing that has improved my putting most since I adopted the cross-handed method is the fact that now my left hand and wrist remain firm and in control. The right hand never 'takes over,' causing the left wrist to collapse at impact. The face of the putter remains square to the line for a longer time without any special effort on my part to keep it square. Thus I now feel I have a better chance of putting the ball along the line I selected."

Johnny Pott uses several individual variations which seem to help his personal putting efficiency. First, he places only two of the fingers of his left hand on the club itself, overlapping the other two over his lower two right fingers. Then he uses a flat-top putter grip, with both thumbs placed on it. He also guards against too strong influence by his right hand, keeping his left hand in control in order to prevent closing the face of the club or pushing the ball on impact.

Both Ellis and Pott have excellent records on the pro tour, and their comments make it clear that the cross-handed grip can be used effectively. They also indicate that the golfer who chooses to experiment with this grip should work out his own variations of its minor details. The same would doubtless be true of both the Runyan-Rodgers split grip and the so-called conventional grip.

(Croquet-style putting is essentially a matter of changing the stance rather than the grip. It will be discussed in the chapter on stance, which follows.)

After the golfer works out his own best method of placing his hands on the club, he must still determine how tightly to grip it. In the opinion of most experts, most average golfers grip the club too tightly, so tightly, in fact, that they set up muscular tension in the fore-arms, ruining their chances of achieving a fluid, smooth putting stroke.

The general advice usually supplied is that the club should be held firmly enough to assure complete control at all times, yet not so firmly as to set up undue tension. Many golfers, beginners in particular, would probably find this advice too vague and need something more specific. Trying to be more graphic, some experts have said that the pressure should approximately equal the amount you would use in holding a small bird in order not to let it get away and yet not to hurt it.

Another problem to be considered is whether gripping pressure should be evenly distributed. Should more pressure be applied with one hand than the other, or should extra pressure be applied with certain fingers? Logic would require your holding the club a bit more firmly with the left hand than the right, since the left hand is used mainly to steady the club and keep it correctly aligned, while the right hand basically propels the clubhead and regulates the force with which the ball is hit. Since you depend chiefly on the right hand for touch, the grip pressure with this hand should be quite delicate. Most experts do agree that the pressure executed by the left hand, particularly the last three fingers, should slightly exceed that exerted by the right.

Bobby Jones, for example, has emphasized the danger of tenseness in a putting grip, maintaining that the left hand alone should firmly grip the club. Jones used only the last three fingers of the left hand to achieve this firmness.

One point easily overlooked is that the gripping muscles will naturally tighten as the clubhead is taken away from the ball and the clubhead's weight begins to be sensed by the controlling muscles. Taking this into account, you should make the grip at address quite light, since it will naturally tighten somewhat as the actual stroke begins.

The golfer who suspects that his putting troubles may stem from his gripping the putter too tightly or too loosely (this latter fault is much more rare) should simply go to the practice green and try out various grip pressures to determine the one that best suits him.

The Grip [83

5. The Stance

AN effective putting stance has three basic, interrelated components:

First, you must stand so that the ball and the hole are in proper perspective. That is, you must be able to look from the ball directly along the line it must travel to reach the hole.

Second, the stance must assure you balance and stability. This ties in with perspective, since if you move (reposition) the body during the stroke, you will not have the same perspective you started with, and consequently will have a different alignment with your target.

Third, you must be as comfortable as possible, while still maintaining proper perspective, balance and stability. Comfort in this case, of course, means the absence of any strain or cramp—the sort that allows

When developing a good putting stance, you should begin with a square stance, where the toes of both feet are on an imaginary line that is parallel to the intended path of the ball.

maximum freedom of movement to the arms and hands while keeping the rest of the body stationary.

Any given putting stance may emphasize one of these components over the other two. For instance, the open stance, in which the right foot is advanced from one to several inches closer to the target line than the left, affords a slightly better perspective because the body more nearly faces the hole. This makes it easier to sight along the intended line by moving the head back and forth.

The Stance [85

In regard to perspective, then, the open is superior to the closed stance. With a closed stance, the right foot is pulled back one to several inches behind the left, which naturally turns the body slightly away from the target. But the closed stance, because it also moves the right hip back, affords more freedom of movement for the arms on the backswing.

The square stance, in which the toes of both feet are on a line parallel with the intended line of the putt, is a compromise between the open and closed stances, embodying, but not emphasizing, the best and worst features of each.

The golfer encounters another problem in deciding on how far apart to place his feet. Spreading the feet wide apart naturally provides better balance and stability. But by doing so he also tends to stretch and tense the muscles of his back and shoulders, thereby taking something away from his sense of touch, or feel.

All this is prefatory to saying that putting stances vary greatly, even among the very best putters, and is intended to explain to some extent why they do. Bill Casper and Bobby Locke, two of the greatest putters that golf has ever known, favor a slightly closed stance. It is probable that both have extraordinary peripheral vision with no problem in scanning the line of their putts and, therefore, prefer to emphasize freedom of movement on the backswing.

Bob Rosburg uses a slightly open stance, but he

Common stance variations used by golfers are the open stance (above), where the front foot is pulled back several inches farther than the back foot from the intended line, and the closed stance (below), where the back foot is pulled several inches farther than the front from the putting line

couples it with a short putting backswing and consequently has no need to be concerned about the right hip getting in the way when he takes the club back.

Johnny Revolta, a super-putter in his prime, adopted a very open putting stance, so open that on especially long putts where he needed to take a long backswing he risked hitting his right foot with the head of his putter. It may be significant that, using this putting stance, he was excellent on short- or medium-range putts but had some trouble on the long approach putts.

Most putting experts use and recommend the square stance. (In his book on putting, Bob Rosburg said he used and advocated a square stance, but he actually advances his right foot an inch or so ahead of his left in a slightly open stance.)

The width of the stance varies enormously among successful putters, from the "spread-eagle" stance of woman pro Ruth Jessen, who places her feet more than a yard apart, to several who place their feet so close together that they almost touch. Bobby Jones, who stressed comfort above all else, favored a very narrow stance, maintaining that he found it the most comfortable. Lloyd Mangrum, a great putter in his prime, stood with his feet not more than half an inch apart. Arnold Palmer's stance is also quite narrow. Bill Casper places his feet about 12 inches apart, which could be designated the medium range. So do Snead, Jerry

The distance between your feet for a good putting stance can vary considerably. Compare Bill Casper's stance (left), where his feet are about 12 inches apart, with Ruth Jessen's spread-eagle stance (below).

Barber, and, in fact, most of the other players on the professional tour.

As noted earlier, a prime consideration in taking the stance is achieving balance and stability. This is what Palmer is seeking by turning both knees inward to brace himself against any possible body movement. The tendency to move the body on the backswing is slight. It is far less a threat than the tendency to move the body laterally in the direction of the hole as the clubhead is started forward to strike the ball, which is a particular danger in tense situations. Anxiety makes it difficult to stand rock steady until the ball is hit and on its way.

Players try to guard against sway in different ways. Jack Nicklaus' solution is to stand with the bulk of his weight on the right foot. To a lesser degree, so does Cary Middlecoff. England's Joyce Wethered also advocated a putting stance in which most of the weight was on the right side.

"The question of stance must be decided," Miss Wethered said, "with a view, first, to finding the best position in which the balance of the body can be controlled. On the whole, it is preferable to keep the weight back on the right foot, and well back on the heels, in order to prevent the dangerous practice of swaying forward during the stroke. It is easier in this way to maintain the necessary tension of the body until the stroke is completed. The important thing to note is that the hold of the feet on the ground determines the steadiness of the body—a vitally necessary form of support when such a very delicate action as putting is being carried out with the hands. No swaying of the upper part of the body must be allowed during the stroke; even after the ball is hit, it is dangerous."

But despite Nicklaus' example and Joyce Wethered's eloquence on the subject, a majority of good putters prefer to stand with more weight on the left side than the right. Casper advocates distributing weight either even on both feet, or with a slight preponderance on the left side. Jerry Barber puts most of his weight on his left side. R. H. "Dick" Sikes, perhaps the best putter among the younger pros, favors the left side to the extent that his right leg seems entirely relaxed, and the bottom of his right foot is completely off the ground.

Arnold Palmer is one of the many who stand with their weight equally distributed on both feet, but he emphasized having the weight to the inside (near the instep) rather than to the outside.

Paradoxical as it may seem, golfers who stand with most of their weight on their left side are also trying to guard against swaying the body laterally in the direction of the hole. They simply view the problem differently from those who favor the right side, reasoning that if the bulk of the weight is on the left side to begin with, there will be less tendency to shift to that direction during the stroke.

The point is that there are excellent putters who elect to stand with the weight on the right side, on the left side, or equally distributed. It is, like so many other things in putting, something that each player must work out for himself.

The same rule applies to width of stance. In this connection, some authorities favor a fairly wide stance for long putts and a narrow one for short putts. In fact, nearly all good putters—Bill Casper is a case in point—

In the Campbell putting method, the golfer moves his right foot to the right various foot-widths, depending on the length of the putt and then takes the putter back even with his right toe. The length of your backstroke determines the distance of your putt.

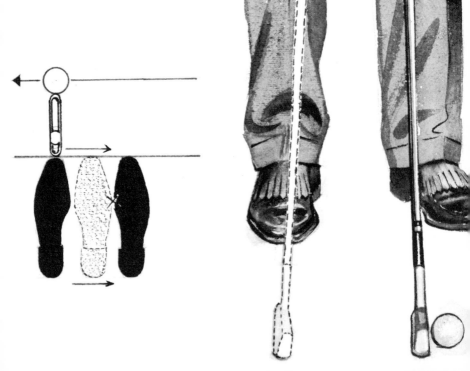

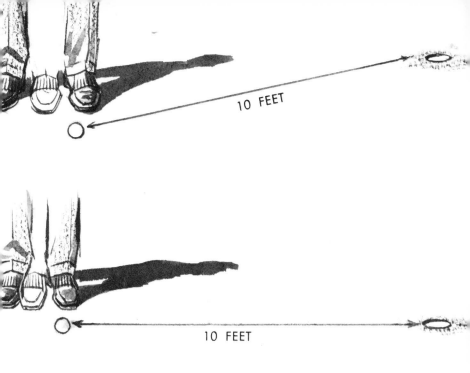

10 FEET

10 FEET

When using the Campbell method, an uphill putt of 10 feet may require the stance width and backstroke length for a level 12-footer. The longer stroke provides the added force needed to get the ball up the inclined putting surface.

widen their basic stance to some degree when the putt is a very long one and a long backswing is required.

Most golfers who alter stance width depending on the length of the putt do so merely on the basis of intuition. But a Philadelphia teaching pro named Rod Campbell claims to have worked the matter out precisely, in fact, he calls his system "precision putting-in." The basic feature of Campbell's method is that the backstroke length is measured by the distance between your left and right foot at address. If, by your own tests, this width represents the backstroke length of a putt needed to give you a 10-foot putt, then twice the width will send your ball 20 feet, and three times the width will send the ball 30 feet. The foot is moved to the right, one width for each added 10-foot-unit of distance desired. It is moved fractional widths in order to achieve distances between multiples of ten feet (e.g. $1\frac{1}{3}$ widths will result in a putt of 13 feet). Another important feature of the Campbell method is a constant stroke tempo.

"Precision putting-in," or some variation of it, might be helpful to some golfers. Campbell says that longtime pro and onetime National Amateur champion Skee Reigel tried it and liked it. But the vast majority of golfers will probably continue to rely on less intricate systems.

Regarding stance and posture, there is one point that virtually all good putters have in common: they stand so that their eyes are directly above the ball. "This makes for better coordination between hands and eyes," says Cary Middlecoff. "If you are bending too far forward so that the eyes will look straight down at a point beyond the ball, your chances of putting consistently well are slim indeed. The same is true if your stance is so upright that you will look straight down at a point between your feet and the ball." Middlecoff adds, "If you find your putting game gone sud-

Arnold Palmer demonstrates how he always positions his eyes directly over the ball when he putts.

denly bad, this is probably the most likely place to look for correction."

Ken Venturi is so convinced of the importance of having the eyes directly over the ball that he sometimes checks himself on this point by holding his putter out at eye level and suspending it directly over the ball. In this way he marks the place where his eyes should be when he takes his stance.

Having the eyes directly over the ball is, of course, quite logical. When scanning the path you want the ball to travel, you obviously want your starting point to be where the ball is now. Getting a proper putting perspective and subsequent stroke is more difficult, if your eyes are focussed anywhere else.

Nearly all good putters also prefer to stand to the ball in a way that allows the upper part of their arms to rest, and thus be steadied against the body. Another vital feature of an effective putting stance is slightly flexed knees. To lock either knee joint, or worse, both of them, would tense the leg muscles, setting up what would certainly be a stiff and uncomfortable stance.

Bobby Jones favored keeping the arms close to the body with a slight bend in both knees. But at least one of today's great putters partially disagrees with the principle of drawing the arms in close to the body and resting them against the sides. Jerry Barber sets his left arm out from his body, with his left elbow pointing in the direction of the hole. And a putting genius of

Keeping your arms in close to your body or away from your body is a matter of personal preference. At top, Jerry Barber shows how he keeps his left arm very far away from his body while his right arm is in close to his side. At bottom is Arnold Palmer's address position with both his arms in close to his sides.

an earlier era defied the principle, altogether. The late Leo Diegel, whose best years were the early 1920's, kept both arms out from the body, with the left elbow pointing toward the hole and the right one pointing in the opposite direction. Diegel's was perhaps the most bizarre putting stance in golf history until the so-called "croquet stance" began to gain some adherents on the pro tour, notably Bob Duden, Jack Rule and Bob Shave.

Writing about putting nearly a half century ago, Joyce Wethered observed: "The player has many difficulties to contend with. He is neither on the same level as the ball, nor behind it, but above and at a peculiarly awkward angle for getting a clear view of the line. These details add very considerably to the difficulty of aiming or striking correctly."

Such concern may well have led to the development of the croquet method. As Miss Wethered suggested, the player cannot get on the same level with the ball (the rules prohibit billiardlike putting). Using the croquet method, the player stands behind the ball, no longer positioning himself "at a peculiarly awkward angle for getting a clear view of the line." He straddles the ball and moves the putter between his legs, as he would a croquet mallet. A specially constructed putter is employed, its shaft joining the center of the clubhead and usually bowed outward.

Dean Refram increased his tour earnings consider-

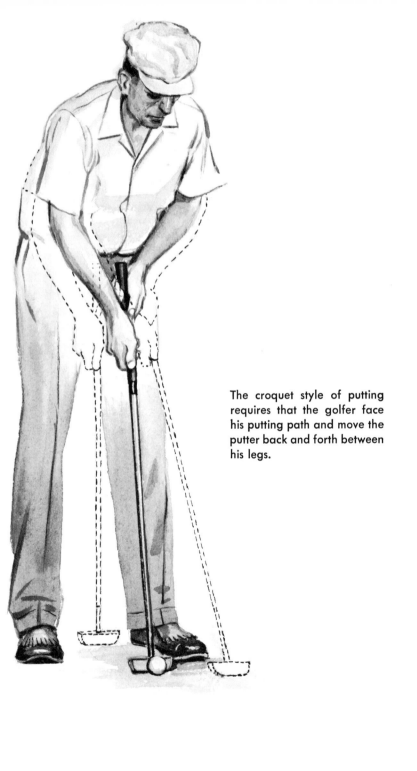

The croquet style of putting requires that the golfer face his putting path and move the putter back and forth between his legs.

ably after he adopted this method. And Duden, another croquet putter, has been described by Cary Middle-coff as "the best downhill putter I ever saw." Others also advocate it as superior to conventional styles.

Critics of the croquet concede that it might be superior for short putts, downhill putts, or on very fast greens—in short, on putts which call for a soft stroke. But they consider it inferior for putts that must be hit hard and therefore require a longer backswing.

Those who approach the problem of putting on a strictly scientific basis may be interested in the results of some research conducted by a South Carolina ophthalmologist, Dr. William W. Vallotton, who is also an avid golfer: "After the head is tilted more than thirteen degrees from the vertical meridian, the cyclo-torsional movements of the eye are unable functionally to rotate the eye. The vertical muscles begin acting as horizontal muscles, and the horizontal muscles as semi-vertical muscles. The inferior oblique muscles, whose overaction occurs in many normal people, are in an optimum position to wreak havoc with the finer fusional components of binocular vision. A mild esophoria or exophoria now becomes a semivertical abnormality, especially when one eye is blocked by a large nose—a transient tropia.

"To circumvent these difficulties putting between the legs, croquet style, is advocated. The type of putter used is the mallet or croquet type. The stance taken can be modified to suit the individual whether both feet are parallel or one foot is in front of the other. This type of putting is now being advocated by several professional golfers."

It can be said, in sum, that putting stances do indeed vary greatly, and the fact that a particular stance works for one golfer is no assurance that it will work for another. Probably the best possible advice is to stick with your present stance if it works for you; if not, try a number of other stances until you find one that seems to suit you.

6. The Stroke

WE come now to the actual striking of the ball with the putter. In considering this phase of the putting process, the player should give thought to three main points:

First, the overall stroke should be smooth, rhythmic, fluid. It should be in no way hurried, jerky, frantic. It should have tempo.

Second, the face of the putter should be square (at right angles) to the intended line of roll when it contacts the ball.

Third, the ball should be struck solidly; contact should be made between the center of gravity of the clubface and the back of the ball.

Setting up a proper tempo is the first thing to be accomplished as you start the stroking process. Having set yourself comfortably over the ball, you make a few small preliminary movements as you scan the line along which you intend to roll the ball. These movements correspond to the waggle, which is the name given the back and forth movements you make preliminary to hitting a longer shot.

Many golfers first set the putterhead behind the ball, then in front of the ball, then behind it again, and from that last movement go into the backswing. Others, waggle the clubhead—either back and forth or up and down, or sometimes both—while keeping the head of the putter always behind the ball. It doesn't matter which of these waggling techniques you use.

What is important is to precede the actual backswing with a certain amount of movement. To stand immobilized over the ball and then go abruptly into the backswing robs you of rhythmic tempo. You will jab or stab your putts instead of stroking them. Casper observes on this point:

"To further insure that my stroke is free of tension and is as rhythmic as possible, I employ a little up-and-down waggle with the putter blade behind the ball. This little maneuver often goes unnoticed, but it has a very definite purpose: that of helping me take the putter blade back as smoothly as possible, and to ensure a proper line to the hole. This movement is actually the beginning of my putting stroke. . . . Other golfers employ similar movements which are largely designed for the same purpose."

As you make these preliminary movements, being

The putting "waggle" helps the golfer achieve a fluid motion during his actual putting stroke. The sequence above illustrates one of several popular prestroke "waggles." After the putter goes behind the ball it then returns to the initial address position before beginning the backstroke.

careful to keep them smooth and unhurried, think of them as leading you into a smooth, unhurried start of the backstroke. Bear in mind that there is a natural tendency to speed up the putting stroke as it goes along, particularly if it is a crucial one, so you certainly don't want to rush your stroke at the start.

All good putters stress the need for a smooth, rhythmic tempo. There is much difference of opinion, however, about whether the tempo should be slow or brisk. Many putters say that the stroke ought to be a "sweep." Other equally skillful putters prefer a brisk "tap," or, as Bob Rosburg describes it, a "pop."

Those who advocate the long sweeping stroke usually cite Bobby Jones as their spokesman. Jones advocated a long stroke, with a sweeping and bowling motion, as contrasted with a sharp stroke hitting down on the ball. He bases this theory on the assumption that a long sweeping motion prevents cutting across the ball or picking up the right hand (which causes cutting). Jones also favors a flat arc for the putter blade.

Some players feel that the Jones method is outmoded. Paul Runyan observes, "Generally speaking, the more sweeping, pendulum stroke of former days (best exemplified by Bobby Jones) . . . has been replaced by a firmer, more compact hit. By and large, the touch putters of my day have disappeared. They were accomplished enough on long approach putts, but from five and six feet today's tappers are much more accurate.

The Stroke [105

Watch Casper, Rosburg or Sanders, and you will see them hit, rather than sweep, the ball."

But the sweep stroke is still favored by many modern players, including Jerry Barber, one of the greatest putters of any era. "I feel strongly," says Barber, "that the stroke should be uninhibited in length. Some players prefer the quick jab or 'pop' style on short putts. However, this method is not effective on long putts. Therefore these players must, in effect, develop two putting techniques. I prefer a smooth, unlimited stroke because it works for me on both short and long putts."

Casper, generally considered the king of the tap putters, agrees with Barber on one point; the tappers do, in fact have to develop two separate techniques. "On short putts up to ten or fifteen feet," says Casper, "the tap method of putting should be used. The clubhead is swung back in a short arc and the ball is struck rather sharply. The movement of the clubhead is slightly downward and through the ball on the follow-through. This brings the clubhead to a stop three or four inches past the ball's position at address. On longer putts, the hands and arms swing back farther on the backswing and the follow-through is longer."

Doug Ford, another of the great putters, uses a short, brisk tap regardless of the length of the putt, although naturally he uses a longer backswing for long putts than for short ones. Bob Rosburg makes no distinction between long and short putts, saying simply, "The stroke is a 'pop.' " But he does concede that the long sweeping stroke can be used with great effectiveness. He notes that Bobby Locke, whom he described as "the best putter in the world when he played the tour in the late 1940's," advocates a flowing pendulum stroke using the arms.

These contrasting views reveal that, regarding tempo, there are two sharply distinct schools of thought. Those who favor a brisk tempo are generally classified as wrist putters (Casper, Rosburg, Ford, et al.). Those who use a longer stroke, and therefore a slower tempo, are called arm-and-shoulder putters (Jones, Locke, Barber, et al.).

Casper, who uses elements of both methods, describes them as follows:

"The wrist method involves primarily the movement of the hands. The arms move very little except on long putts, but the hands are quite active because of the hinging action of the wrists.

"In the arm-and-shoulder style of putting the wrists are frozen, so to speak, and the basic movement comes from the arms and shoulders. The hands are regarded as being part of the shaft and the wrists are locked firmly in place from start to finish, except for extremely long putts, when the wrists are permitted to break slightly."

But a word of warning probably should be injected here lest the reader feel he must make an absolutely clear distinction and elect one style or the other, exclusively. "Of course, these are matters of shading," says

The Stroke [107

The wrist method of putting involves very little movement from any part of the body other than the hands. Note how the wristbreak in the right hand controls the backstroke.

Runyan. "A tap can be overshortened or hurried into a jab. And if you take the wrists out of the stroke too grimly you can stiffen up too much. Any good point can be overdone."

If you overdo the wrist method, you may frequently find yourself snatching the clubhead back too hurriedly on the backswing. Then what you had intended as a putting stroke will become a frantic jab or stab. If you overdo the arm-and-shoulder technique, you may find yourself drawing the club back so far on the backswing that you have to decrease your tempo as you bring the clubhead back into the ball. In either case, you fail to achieve the desired rhythm, smoothness, and fluidity.

Whether you use the wrist method or the arm-and-shoulder method, you will still need to be certain that the clubhead is accelerating as it comes into the ball, not slowing down.

"If the backswing becomes too long, the stroke must necessarily be softened coming through in order to stop the ball from going too far," says Runyan. "Such deceleration takes away the tap which gives a putt firmness."

Bob Rosburg is even more emphatic on this point. "Try always to hit the ball with the clubhead accelerating at impact," he advises. "It is very difficult to hit the ball solidly if the clubhead is losing speed as it approaches the ball. This usually happens when you change your mind midway through the swing. If that occurs, the clubhead tends to waver in midstroke and all

For the arm-and-shoulder putting style, the wrists break very little. The putting stroke stems from the pendulum movement of the arms and shoulders.

chances of a solid hit are gone. The last thing I think of before the swing is acceleration of the clubhead before impact."

The essence of good putting stroke tempo (timing) is, then, to have the clubhead gradually gaining speed as it comes into the ball, which is also the essence of good timing on swings for all other shots.

Our second basic stroke principle requires that the face of the putter be square with the intended line of roll when the ball is struck. If the face is open (turned outward) when the ball is hit, the putt will go to the right of the intended line. A closed face at impact will send the ball to the left. The square-face principle can be departed from successfully only if the player deliberately aligns himself to the right or left of his target with intent to compensate by pushing or pulling the putt. A player who does this cannot logically hope to be a successful putter.

The square face at impact is what is contemplated in gripping the club with the back of the left hand facing the line and the back of the right hand opposing it. The intention is to have the hand (and thus the face of the putter) in the same position at impact as at the start of the stroke, and the simplest way to bring this about, is to oppose the hands directly to begin with.

The stance, too, is designed to help attain this same end. We have found that comfort, balance and sta-

The Stroke [111

If the face of the putter is closed, the ball must go to the left of the hole.

the face of the putter is
open, the ball must go to
the right of the hole.

The most vital element for successful putting is to be sure to line up the face of your putter perfectly square to the intended path of the ball.

bility should be its essential features. If the stance position is awkward or strained, or if there is body movement during the stroke, the difficulty of bringing the clubhead squarely into the ball is increased.

This principle leads, naturally and logically, to the backswing.

"The putting stroke should be as simple as possible," says Casper. "The simpler the stroke, the more effective and consistent it will be under pressure." On this point, there is no argument at all among the experts, whether they be wrist putters or arm-and-shoulder putters.

The wrist putters strive for simplicity by making the shortest possible stroke that will still generate the power (clubhead speed) necessary to knock the ball to the hole. They reason that the shorter the stroke, the less is apt to go wrong with it.

The arm-and-shoulder putters seek simplicity by keeping wrist break to a minimum. It is obvious that to whatever extent the wrists are cocked on the back-swing, they must uncork by that same amount on the forward swing, if the face of the putter is to be square with the line at impact. So if the wrists are largely kept out of the stroke, a longer backswing is required.

It might appear that the ideal putting backswing would carry the clubhead back from the ball in an ab-solutely straight line. This would be true, however, only if the stroke were started with the hands directly over the ball, with the shaft of the putter perfectly perpendicular to the ground. Then a true pendulum stroke could be achieved, but it would be an awkward and unnatural stroke.

In the normal address position, the hands are held close to the body, setting up an angle of inclination between the hands and the ball. The idea is to maintain the same angle of inclination (plane) on the backswing. In doing this, the clubhead naturally moves a bit inside the line, and the clubface will appear to be slightly open when you reach the end of the backswing. But if you have stayed on the correct plane, the clubface will still be square to the ball. It is the same principle that Ben Hogan emphasizes with reference to the full golf swing. The putting backswing plane is less noticeable, however, because it is much more steeply inclined than the backswing plane in the case, for example, of the driver. Nevertheless, the plane is there and should be adhered to.

In the correct and simple putting stroke, the path of the clubhead on the forward swing simply retraces the path it took on the backswing. This is natural, uncomplicated and requires no adjustments to bring the clubhead into the ball with the face square to the line. You simply go through the ball with the back of the left hand facing the line, as it was when you started the stroke. As a margin of safety, you should keep the back of the left hand facing down the line for a few more inches after the ball is hit.

The stroke path of the forward swing should retrace the path of the backswing on all putts.

Bobby Jones considered the follow-through of the left wrist and arm the first requirement of a good putting motion. Bob Rosburg, while stating it slightly differently, is in essential agreement: "The right hand should never pass the left until well after the ball has been struck."

While experts generally agree that in a sound putting stroke the left hand dominates the action on the back-

A sound principle that many good putters agree on is that on the backswing the left hand should push the putter away from the ball (top), and on the downswing the right hand should take over and push the clubhead into the ball (bottom).

swing and the right hand on the forward swing, at the same time, they warn against too much conscious emphasis on this point. They counsel against saying to yourself, "I'm going to take the club back with my left hand and hit the ball with my right," because that sort of thinking prohibits your making a smooth, continuous putting stroke in which both hands play their proper roles naturally and spontaneously.

Similar reasoning underlies opinion on taking the putter back low to the ground. Both the sweep putters

To achieve a firm putting stroke and a smooth roll of the ball on the putting surface, keep the putter low to the ground throughout its backward and forward movement.

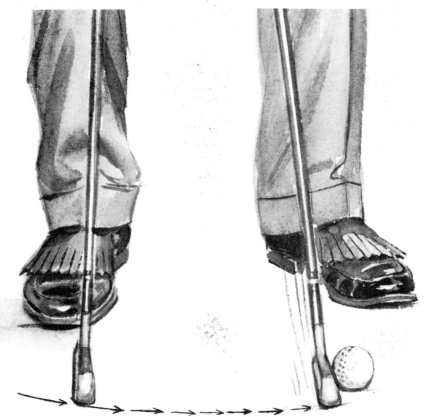

and the tap putters advocate low backstroking as opposed to picking the clubhead up abruptly, but emphasize once again that a low backstroke is something that should come naturally in the development of a sound putting stroke.

The third basic stroking principle is that the ball must be hit solidly.

"According to my lengthy and close observations," says Cary Middlecoff, "one point held in common by all good putters is that they hit the ball solidly. They almost always bring the center of the clubface into contact with the center of the ball. This has to be an ironclad rule of good putting, because hitting the ball solidly is the only way that 'touch'—the unconscious ability to hit the ball at the desired speed, or momentum—can be achieved. The putter who tends to hit the ball off center must on some occasions hit it more off center than on others, and will now and then, by chance, hit it center. Thus he can never be sure of the amount of force he is getting behind the ball, power being a combination of clubhead speed, clubhead weight, and meeting the ball squarely."

"Try to hit the ball solidly," says Bob Rosburg. "That is one of my principal putting theories."

"Perfect cleanness of striking is now sought after before any other consideration," Joyce Wethered maintained. "The ball perfectly hit so that it rolls without any sideway spin will, with remarkable regularity, disappear from view, and practically on that expectation present calculations are based." As Miss Wethered indicates, the ball solidly struck will roll without any sideway spin, and, by the same reasoning, a ball hit off center will to some degree spin sideways. Miss Wethered elaborates on the theory of the solid hit:

"The object that should be aimed at in striking the ball is to hit it in such a way that it runs toward the hole on a horizontal axis and is free from any sideway spin. 'Rolling' the ball quite smoothly in putting—to turn it, as it were, on an even keel—is not quite as simple a matter as it looks, because there is an insidious tendency to turn it on the axis corresponding with the angle of the shaft of the club, which it makes in relation to the ground, and to give it the slight sidespin which is known as 'cutting' the ball."

Bill Casper is equally emphatic, but hardly so technical. "Learn to roll the ball," he advises, noting that his friend Rosburg rolls the ball especially well because he hits it solidly.

Chief among the several things that contribute to consistently solid hitting of putts is riveting the eyes on the back of the ball and keeping them there until the ball is hit and on its way. Coordination between putterface and ball is paramount. You have to look at the ball.

Second, there must be no body movement during

the stroke, as was noted in the section on stance. If the body moves, the head inevitably moves with it, and the eyes cannot remain focused on the ball. Also when the body shifts, the position of the hands with reference to the ball will alter, which will make solid contact considerably more difficult to attain.

Third, you must be consistent in your positioning of the ball with reference to the feet. If you play the ball off the left toe at one time, opposite the left instep at another, and occasionally back near the right foot, you cannot set up a consistent stroking pattern.

Virtually all experts agree that the ball should be positioned on a line with the left instep. The ball then lies at the point where, in the natural course of the forward swing, the head of the putter is traveling parallel with the ground. You should avoid hitting down on the ball, which tends to send it skidding along with some underspin on it instead of rolling straight over and over, and you should likewise avoid hitting the ball with the face of the putter traveling upward, which may lift the ball rather than roll it.

It should be said, however, that there have been some successful putters, notably Lloyd Mangrum, who tended to hit down on the ball, and there have been some very good ones who have hit the ball with a slight upward motion as a means of producing extra overspin. But these tactics are certainly exceptions to the general rule; you might even call them idiosyncrasies.

The average golfer would undoubtedly be wiser to build his technique around a solid hit in which the head of the putter moves along level with the top of the grass.

A point that is emphasized by a number of ace golfers, including Cary Middlecoff and Bill Casper, is that the putting stroke ought basically to be the same for every putt—a repeating stroke. Only the amount of power applied should vary.

Middlecoff believes it is better to have an essentially unsound putting stroke that you can repeat each time than to be inconsistent with a basically sound stroke. He cites the case of Dave Douglas: "Dave cut all his putts. He took the putter back outside the line and cut right across the ball, which is against all the principles of good putting. He always had the ball spinning a little from left to right. It just seemed to be natural for him to hit it that way. But he always hit it the same way, and he was a good putter for that reason alone."

Casper strongly advocates—and uses—an "orderly procedure" on the greens. He establishes and follows a set pattern for each putt, even to the extent of taking approximately the same amount of time to select his line. Then he steps briskly up to the ball, takes two practice swings (no more and no less) and then strokes the putt. Clearly, his orderly procedure is aimed at maintaining a repeating stroke.

The Stroke [123

Bobby Locke is another who has a set putting pattern, almost a ritual. He and Casper are much alike in this respect, the chief difference between them being that Locke takes three practice swings to Casper's two.

A recurring feature of Casper's orderly procedure, and of Locke's near-ritual, is positioning the ball identically each time, and always getting that solid hit.

Achieving a solid hit is especially important when you putt from off the putting surface—from the fringe of the green, or from a short way out on the fairway, or even, occasionally, from a level lie in a shallow sand trap that has no overhanging bank. There are shots in which "touch" is a prime consideration. In these situations the first stage of your putt will be over terrain rougher than the putting surface. Since you can expect that the ball may be thrown uncontrollably a bit off line, your main concern will be to apply enough force to the ball to counteract the effects of the terrain. You should therefore be particularly careful to keep your attention on the back of the ball and your mind centered on hitting the ball solidly.

A word that has come to be closely associated with the putting stroke is "yips," an all-purpose and ugly little word that fits just about all the things that can go wrong with a putting stroke. "Yips" seems to afflict older golfers and, in a general way, is associated with jumpy nerves, but young golfers are by no means immune to it. It hasn't really been established whether the player gets the putting yips because he has jumpy nerves or vice versa.

This affliction is rather a touchy subject among the pros, particularly among those who happen to be in the throes of the yips, or who have recently been, or who fear that the yips might strike at any time. Cary Middlecoff agreed, however, to attempt a description:

"A player with the putting yips is just somebody who, temporarily at least, is a real bad putter. He may have had a sound putting stroke and lost it, or he may have had a flaw in his stroke that finally caught up with him—like hooding the face of the putter going back. But it could be anything, any one of a lot of things. Being too quick starting the backswing, for instance, and getting quicker and jerkier as you go along.

"I really think the people who hood the face of the putter going back think they are keeping the face square to the line. They either neglect the principle of the plane of the swing—the fact that the shaft of the putter is slanted outward to start with—or they don't understand it, don't get the picture of it. To hood the face, you have to turn the wrists back to the left some as you go back. It's the same as the shut-face swing, like Arnold Palmer's. You think you're keeping the clubface square to the ball (or to the line, whichever way you want to put it) but you're not.

"The face is closed, and if you close the face going back you've sure got to open it coming into the ball

In the 1966 PGA Championship at the Firestone C.C., Sam Snead resorted to a very unusual variation of the croquet putting style and, by doing so, stayed in contention throughout the tournament.

to get the face square at impact. And naturally it gets to be a question of whether you open it enough to get it square or open it too much and have it open. You're guessing. And a given number of wrong guesses will give you the yips.

"But I think that most bad putts are caused by indecision. The player doesn't fully make up his mind how he wants to stroke the putt, so he changes his mind somewhere between the start of the backswing and the end of the forward swing. He decides that he ought to play for more break, or for less break, so he changes his stroke pattern. Or maybe the thought hits him that he is about to hit the ball too hard or too soft, so he slows down or speeds up his stroke. The result is a wavering, indecisive stroke, and this kind of stroke makes very few putts. You must make up your mind in advance how you're going to stroke the ball, and stick to your plan. When the mind wavers, the stroke wavers, and a wavering stroke won't do the job.

"Another danger to guard against during the stroke is becoming too anxious to see where the ball goes. Anxiety can, if you let it, make you raise your head before the ball is hit, which is fatal. The good putters don't raise their heads until the ball is partway along the line to the cup. They keep the head firmly in place and follow the first stages of the putt by just turning their eyes in the direction of the hole after the ball is hit.

"Some players don't watch the ball at all, but just hit it and listen to find out if the ball went into the cup. I think this is a good technique to use in practice, to form the habit of keeping your eyes on the ball and your head still, but in actual play it's very hard on the nerves."

The Stroke [127

7. Equipment

MANY golfers believe that some-
where in the world there is one putter which, above
all others, would be the best for them. They keep
searching for it. They never pass a putter rack in a
pro shop or a store without handling and critically ex-
amining everything in stock. They also take putters
out of other people's bags and waggle them a few times
before replacing them. If a putting green is handy, or
a rug, they conduct a brief test.

Some buy many different types of putters and keep
them on hand for experimental purposes. Curtis Person, a Memphis amateur and frequent winner of sen-
ior tournaments, seldom owns fewer than two dozen
putters, and during his career has owned or borrowed
perhaps several thousand of them. The trunk of almost
any touring pro's car probably contains no fewer than
half a dozen putters, and probably more.

Most pro shops and sporting goods outlets selling golf clubs display a variety of putters so that a golfer can select the one best suited to his or her requirements.

Other golfers feel that the putter they have is generally suited to them. They plan to use it as long as it seems to work or until they just happen to find something they think would work better.

A few golfers swear that the putter they already have, and that they may have loved, owned and treasured for years, is the best one in the world. They couldn't conceive of parting with it.

Many golfers are convinced that a mallet-head-type putter is best. Others vouch for a regular blade-type putter. Still others prefer something center-shafted.

We might, for instance, on a given day in a major tournament find in the same threesome Bill Casper, Art Wall, and Gene Littler. Casper would probably be using a steel-shafted mallet-head which he had tested thoroughly and liked, but which he would exchange for something essentially similar if he saw any reason to do so. Wall would certainly be putting with the old hickory-shafted blade that he has used for 20 years or more. Littler might be using a center-shafted, bronze- or brass-headed putter that he had picked up that morning. All of them would probably be putting somewhere between good and phenomenal.

There are a number of conclusions to be drawn. One is that the selection of a putter is a personal matter. Another is that it is not so much a matter of the particular putter, or even the type of putter, that counts, but rather of the player manipulating it. We

The PGA touring pros have their personal tastes as to the putters they use. (Top left) Bill Casper uses a mallet putter extremely successfully. (Top right) Arnold Palmer has won many PGA tournaments with his flanged blade putter. (Bottom left) PGA champion Gene Littler wins his share of tournaments with a center-shafted putter. (Bottom right) When his orthodox putting touch left him in 1966, Sam Snead found his way to the tournament pay window with a croquet putter.

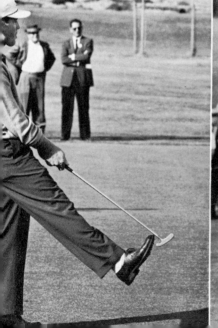

should not, however, conclude that there are not sound principles upon which to base our choice of a putter, because all the experts agree that there are—including those mentioned above, as well as a host of others. As Bill Casper puts it:

"There are several important things to consider when selecting a putter. First of all, it should 'feel' good to you. Second, it should be balanced properly. You should be able to tell if the putter has good feel and balance merely by swinging it back and forth a few times, and hitting a few balls with it on the practice green. Careful attention also should be given to the weight and lie of the putter, as well as to shaft length.

"Select a putter that is easy to line up and easy to look at. Although putting styles have changed little over the years, many new putters have been added to the golf-equipment line. You shouldn't have too much trouble finding a putter to suit your particular needs and putting habits if you spend a little time looking over the various models."

Among the specifics Casper mentions are lie, weight, and shaft length. So let's look first at these three considerations.

The lie is the angle of inclination between the head and the shaft, measured with the sole (bottom) of the putter lying flat on a level surface. The average angle of inclination is about 65 degrees. A putter with that approximate angle between head and shaft would be

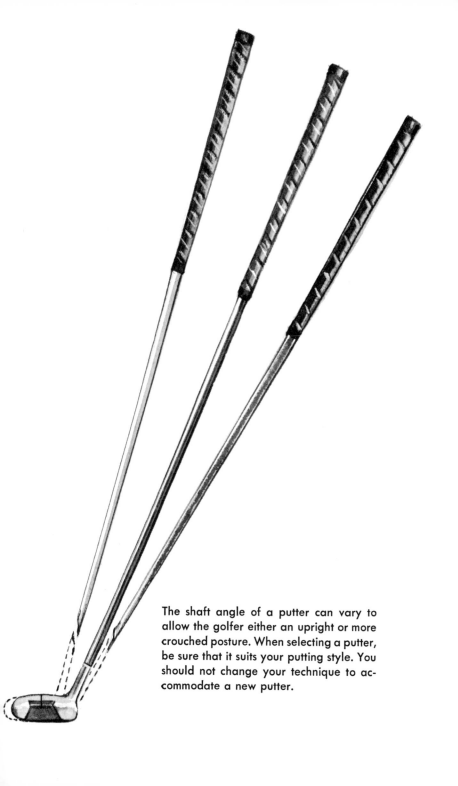

The shaft angle of a putter can vary to allow the golfer either an upright or more crouched posture. When selecting a putter, be sure that it suits your putting style. You should not change your technique to accommodate a new putter.

said to have a medium lie. An angle of, say, 72 degrees would put the putter into the flat-lie classification, and an angle in the 55 degree range would give the putter an upright lie. Putters are, of course, available nowadays with any head-shaft angle you specify.

There is no real need, however, to know about specific angles, or even about the three general classifications of lies, because a set of simple tests will tell you what you want to know. Make the first test standing on a level surface. Take the putter and stand to the ball as you normally would to putt, comfortably situated, with your eyes directly over the ball and your hands as you would usually place them. If the sole of the putter is approximately flush with the surface on which you are standing, the lie is basically right for you.

But you need to make two other tests, because you will not always be putting on a level surface. Sometimes you will stand with your feet on a higher level than the ball (right-breaking putts), and sometimes with your feet on a lower level than the ball (left-breaking putts). For these putts you will have to adjust your stance position in order to reach the ball naturally and comfortably—feet closer to the ball for a right-breaking putt, feet a bit farther from the ball for a left-breaking putt. In making these stance adjustments, you will naturally decrease or increase the head-shaft angle.

You will notice that when you have to stand a bit closer to the ball, the toe of the putter will be flush with the ground but the heel will be slightly raised. Conversely, when you have to stand a bit farther away, the heel of the putter will be flush with the ground and the toe raised slightly. You will observe that a putter with an upright lie would be better for right-breaking putts and a flat-lie putter would suit better for left-breakers.

To be somewhat technical about it, you change the center of gravity of your putter when you change its head-shaft angle. The so-called "sweetspot" (which is the spot on the face of the putter where the ball must be contacted to get an absolutely solid hit) will be moved slightly. When you move the putter more upright, you move the sweetspot nearer the toe. When you widen the head-shaft angle, you move the sweetspot nearer the heel.

To be practical you shouldn't carry three different putters around with you and switch from one to another depending on the type of putt you have. What you need is an all-purpose putter, one that seems to set approximately right whether the putt is a level one or a right- or left-breaker.

One simple test might be termed the "coin-tapping" method. Holding up the putter with thumb and forefinger, you tap with a coin along the face of the putter. When you reach the sweetspot, your thumb and forefinger holding up the club will no longer feel vibration from the tapping. Normally, the sweetspot area is located just behind the center of the club face.

To complete testing your putter's lie, hit a few breaking putts with it. On the right-breakers, contact the ball a little nearer the heel of the club than you have found the sweetspot to be. On the left-breakers, make the contact a little nearer the toe. If you keep getting solid hits, the lie is correct for you.

Most players like the sweetspot to be in the center of the face, or quite near it. But Jim Ferrier, a fine putter over the years, prefers to hit all his putts out nearer the toe of the club, so he has his putters specially weighted to locate the center of gravity in that area.

As to putter weight, the norm is from 15 to 18 ounces, with the head accounting for not quite two-thirds of the overall weight. Shaft lengths run from about 33 to 36 inches. Unless you are of highly exceptional build, the weight and length in the ranges specified above should be right for you. If you exceed these limits, you should understand that you are going against what years of experience have revealed to be essentially correct. Most pros use a 35-inch shaft length and an overall weight of 16 or 17 ounces.

Clubface loft is another important consideration. Casper has this to say on the subject:

"The question of loft has been a matter of contro-

Knowing where the "sweetspot" of your putter is located will help you develop a firmness in your putting stroke. Although the "sweetspot" of most putters is located near the center of the clubface (top), occasionally it is distributed at the toe (center) and sometimes at the heel (bottom) of the putterhead.

versy for years. About the only thing the experts are agreed on is this: there must be loft built into the putter face.

"Just how much loft is a matter of dispute, but I believe it largely depends on the types of greens upon which you are playing. If the greens in your section of the country are rough and slow, then you must definitely use a more lofted putter. This will enable the ball to 'move up' and ride high on the grass immediately upon leaving the putter head. If you used a putter with little or no loft on greens that are out rather high, the ball would be driven into the blades of grass instead of on top of them, thus causing it to hop and jump on its way to the hole.

"If the greens in your area are smooth and fast, then you will need a putter with less loft. An experienced golfer, or your club professional, can tell you about how much loft there is on a putter.

"I would say that a putter with from three to four degrees of loft is suitable for all types of greens. If the greens are extremely fast, then find a putter with a little less loft to it. One of the major manufacturers of putters has determined that a putter with two-and-a-half to three degrees of loft will give the ball the best and most consistent spin off the face of the club."

In this connection, it should be noted that Bobby Jones' famed "Calamity Jane" putter had a face loft

The immortal Bobby Jones' "Calamity Jane" is probably golf's most famous putter. A blade putter with a wooden shaft, "Calamity Jane" was unerring in the hands of the Grand Slam champion.

of 8 degrees, which is close to the average driver face loft of 10 to 11 degrees.

Another point to consider is that you should be able to see the face of your putter as you look down from the position of address, which you can do best with a fairly lofted putter, and which you could hardly do if the face did not slant back at all.

Bob Rosburg sums up his putter-selection theories as follows:

"What kind of putter is best? The one in the most confident hands. Professionals and top amateurs alike use a mixture of mallets and blade-type putters. No one type seems to be more successful than another. The main factor is the mental attitude of the player at the end of the stick.

"Over the years, there has been great progress in design of putters, just as with other clubs. However, I think the recent race to invent and market new kinds of putters has turned into a ridiculous competition of gimmicks.

"The choice of putters is almost unlimited under United States Golf Association rules. The rules specify only that the distance from the heel to the toe must be greater than that from front to back, but they allow bent shafts, flat grips, round heads, and countless other variations."

[With respect to grips, the same U.S.G.A. rules apply as for all other clubs. The rule—2-2F—states: "The grip shall be a continuation of the shaft to which material may be added for the purpose of obtaining a firm hold. The grip shall be substantially straight and plain in form, may have flat side, but shall not have a channel or furrow or be molded for any part of the hands. A device designed to give the player artificial aid in gripping or swinging the club shall be deemed to violate this rule even though it be part of the club."]

"Virtually every putter ever made falls into one of two categories, the mallet and the blade. We might add a third—the croquet style—but this type is relatively rare even though it does provide certain advantages.

"Both major types come in two variations: a standard shaft connecting at the heel of the head, and one connecting near the center of the head. Either shaft may be goose-necked just above where it reaches the clubhead.

"Like cars and clothes, popularity of putters seems to run in streaks. The fad changes from time to time. Currently, the most popular among the professionals seems to be a blade type with a small flange running along the lower half of the back. It usually has a straight shaft connecting at the heel, but center shafts are also popular.

"I've used all kinds of putters at one time or another. I occasionally experiment with different types just to try and regain my touch. But a Tommy Armour blade putter with the flange on the back has been my favorite since my amateur days at Stanford University. This style, with its goose-neck shaft, seems to help me keep my hands ahead of the clubhead in a solid, set position. The whole thing seems to look good when I stand over the ball.

"Arnold Palmer uses this type of putter and has done well with it, to say the least. Ken Venturi, Lionel Hebert, Fred Hawkins, Jack Nicklaus and Johnny Pott have used the same type of putter, with varying degrees of success.

"The bull's-eye type with a center shaft is a variation of my favorite. It feels good to me, but I putt erratically with it. This may be because the blade looks shorter to me when I stand over the ball than does the type where the shaft connects at the heel. But Gene Littler does all right with a bull's-eye. Don January, Mike Souchak, and Billy Maxwell have won lots of money using the same kind. Gary Player uses a bull's-eye much of the time.

"The old-fashioned blade putter, like Bobby Jones' 'Calamity Jane,' still has some fans. It's uncomplicated, which tends to reduce tension when you stand over the ball. However, the center of gravity is usually too high. This tends to make the ball bounce off the clubface instead of rolling smoothly. But an old, wooden-shafted blade has been Art Wall's favorite for years and helped him win the 1959 Masters Tournament and Vardon Trophy for low scoring average. Two more of the world's best players, Bobby Locke and Doug Sanders, have also used the simple blade to win many championships. They all say they have more feel with this type.

"Then there's the mallet. Manufacturing imagination has turned out a great many kinds of mallets. The shape you use should be strictly according to your taste. Heads are usually made of steel or an aluminum alloy, sometimes of wood. Players who use them say they derive a better feel and more confidence from the large clubhead. They don't have to hit the ball as hard, either, which is a great advantage on slow greens.

"Bill Casper uses a mallet and he's the best. But he might do just as well with a blade. Doug Ford, Bruce Crampton, Bob Goalby and Julius Boros putt with mallets. Dow Finsterwald is the only one I know who uses a mallet with a wooden shaft.

"Most croquet putters have a bent shaft, enabling the player to get his hands well in front of the clubhead. This makes it very effective on downhill putts. But 'distance' putting uphill is conversely difficult; you have to hit up on the ball and it is difficult not to top the ball when trying to hit it hard.

"Odd putters usually have disadvantages that offset any advantages. Some of unusual designs eliminate a great margin of error because the ball goes the same if hit anywhere on the face. But I find such putters, with their strange looks, different balance, and, often, odd noise at impact, cut down on my day-in, day-out effectiveness.

"I like a steel clubhead. Steel has a nice hard feel when you hit the ball. I have a lot of trouble hitting the ball hard enough, and steel seems to help me achieve a more solid impact.

"However, brass is a very popular material for putterheads, particularly for small blades. It has a softer feel to it than steel. A lot of people like that 'live' feeling a 'soft-headed' putter provides. I don't.

"One thing some people find helpful is a line or a mark on top of the clubhead to help center the ball on the blade and help square up the face with the hole. I've never cared whether a putter had markings on top or not. I have enough trouble trying to hit the ball correctly without watching lines.

"Putters with colored heads seem to me to be more decorative than practical, but that's just another matter of preference.

"With a new putter made of shiny steel or brass it's a good idea to put a piece of black tape on top so it doesn't shine in your eyes or shoot off funny reflections. But older pieces of metal will be darker in color and won't give you that problem.

"Most pros use a much stiffer shaft than the normal one you would find in the stock of pro-shop putters. Again, the reason is to give the ball a much more solid hit without its springing off the clubhead. A limber shaft makes the ball come off much faster, a feeling that most good players don't like in a putter. Steel shafts are most prevalent. The old hickory or wooden shafts are not too popular any more, largely because they vary in changing climatic conditions. However, quite a few players have switched to the new glass shaft, which consistently has a very soft feel.

"Bent shafts are a fine idea in theory. They put your hands and the clubhead at a better angle in relation to the center of gravity and make it harder to open the clubface. But, like the croquet mallet, the unusual feel of a bent-shaft putter makes the rest of the clubs in your bag feel strange.

"Shaft length is a matter of preference. Most pros use a thirty-five-incher. Just don't get a shaft so short that you bend too much over the ball. This is not natural and creates unnecessary tension.

"Most professionals use regular round leather grips on their putters. Some have gone in for form-fitted rubber or composition grips. There is also the so-called pistol grip which curves in slightly toward the player's body. This is mostly a personal preference in feel when placing the hands on the club.

"Personally, I prefer a rounded, soft-feeling leather grip. One problem with leather, as compared with a rubber-composition grip, is that you must keep it well conditioned to maintain its softness. I've tried flat-top grips but they just don't seem right for my hands. They are a help, though, for a player who wants to get his thumbs side by side on top of the grip.

"The diameter of the grip doesn't really make much difference. The size of the hands in relation to the grip is not much of a factor in putting.

"If you are buying a putter for the first time, or have given up on your old one, start by carefully looking over the practically unlimited styles that are sure to be in your pro shop. First, pick one that looks good. Some golfers prefer the graceful blade, while others like the more forceful mallet.

"If you want to change putters, try using one styled completely differently from your present one. Once you decide on a specific style you can order one with the shaft length, flex, blade lie and grip best suited for you."

Bill Casper notes that most players who use the brisk tap stroke, like himself, prefer stiff-shafted putters. Cary Middlecoff, who takes rather a long putting backswing, likes a shaft that is stiff enough to have no play in it at all on short putts, but which flexes a little on long putts in order to help get the ball up to the hole.

Ralph Guldahl, one of the real greats of a generation ago, liked a shaft so rigid that you couldn't even bend it over your knee.

Just as tastes differ widely in the selection of putters, so do theories on whether to change putters often, seldom, or almost never. The trend among the pros nowadays is toward fairly frequent changes, with the exception of Art Wall's loyalty to the rusty relic that he has used so long and so well. Many players feel that a change in putters will give them a fresh outlook on the whole putting problem. Some change after any single round during which they putt badly.

Against the fresh-outlook theory, you can set the perhaps more logical line of reasoning that the longer you keep a putter, and the more familiar you become with its feel and hitting characteristics, the better it will serve you.

Dow Finsterwald notes that nearly all the tour pros keep more than one putter available for the different types of greens they encounter in various sections of the country. Following a similar theory, the player who customarily plays on his home course might like to have more than one so he can vary his selection depending on whether the greens are fast or slow on a given day. Once more, it is a matter of personal preference.

8. Practice

GARY PLAYER recalls that when he was a youngster in South Africa developing the golf game that was eventually to bring him all four of the world's major championships and a large number of lesser ones, he would practice putting for approximately two hours a day, about a third the over-all time he devoted to working on his golf.

If Player were starting over again, he would devote even more time to his putting practice. It is well known among the touring professionals that Player believes at least half of the aspiring golfer's practice time should be devoted to putting, basing his reasoning on the simple fact that a top player putts approximately as many times as he makes all other shots combined. Assurance of his putting proficiency also affords greater confidence and better morale to sustain other aspects of his game.

Player has doubtless noticed, too, that three of the very finest putters on the tour—Jerry Barber, Art Wall, and Dow Finsterwald—are the three who practice putting the most.

No playing professional doubts the value of putting practice. In fact, it probably would be safe to say that no player could succeed on the tour if he didn't keep his putting touch sharp through practice.

Another point on which the pros are in virtually unanimous accord is that putting pratice should be conducted along definite lines, with a precise goal in mind. They feel that it does little or no good to spend time on the practice putting green thoughtlessly banging the ball toward a hole. One who has developed an orderly procedure and who recommends its use to others is Bill Casper, whom most of his colleagues regard as the best of today's putters.

"Begin by practicing the short putts first," says Casper. "Drop several balls on the putting green about two feet from the holes. Tap them briskly into the hole, concentrating on the speed, not the line, since the line is easy to judge on short putts. After you have putted several minutes from the two-foot range, move back to the three-foot range. Then putt from four feet, five feet, and so on up to ten feet. You should select a flat putting surface for this exercise so that you can learn to judge distances properly. Putts that break should be practiced only after you hit straight putts of varying distances.

"Another common drill for putting the short ones is to first place a number of balls in a circle around the hole. Start at about three or four feet out and work around the clock, tapping each putt firmly toward the hole. After you have putted around the clock from this distance, extend the circle two or three feet farther out and go through the same procedure.

"One of the best methods of practicing long putts," Casper adds, "is to visualize an imaginary circle around the hole about three feet in diameter. Drop several balls about fifteen feet away from the hole and try to roll the ball into the imaginary circle around the hole. Next, drop back to about twenty-five or thirty feet and go through the same routine.

"The important thing to remember here is to concentrate on stroking the ball the desired distance. Too many long putts are left short of the hole because the golfer has concentrated so much on the line that by the time he begins the stroke he has forgotten how hard to hit the ball."

Most experts agree with Casper that the best putting practice routine begins with short putts and works up to long ones. Jerry Barber, however, spends most of his practice time on the long putt, because, he claims, it better helps him to develop touch. There is virtually unanimous agreement that the main aim of putting practice is to develop a sense of feel for the power needed to hit the ball the correct distance. Cary Middlecoff, among others, advocates devoting a portion of your practice time merely to stroking a few putts along the green, rather than toward a cup. "This way you can perfect your touch and smooth out your stroke by concentrating on the cause rather than the result," says Middlecoff.

The late Horton Smith said he found it helpful to stick a wooden tee in the ground and putt at that rather than toward a hole. It was his view that you could improve your putting by using a smaller target in practice than you would have in actual play.

Smith was also a firm advocate of home practice putting—carpet putting. "I will tell you that practice during the off season will pay off a hundred times over in the achievement of better results in the spring," he insisted, "and will provide you with self-satisfaction at the accomplishment of a very worthwhile end.

"Even I will admit that until the invention of ball-return mechanisms it was not much fun to practice putting on the carpet at home. But now the irritation of chasing the errant ball under the easy chair has been ended.

"There are also types of carpet that can be put down over your own floor that simulate very closely the usual surface of a golf green. Another important factor about carpet putting is that with very few outside distractions, you are able, for the time being, to forget about whether you are sinking your putts or whether you are up to or short of the cup, and can concentrate on the most important phase of your putting game—your stroke. That is to say, you can focus on your stroking technique to an extent completely impossible on the regular practice green.

"Work toward a 'discriminating' touch, one that can distinguish between a three-foot putt and a three-and-a-half-foot putt. I cannot overemphasize the importance of this, for it is here that you achieve the ability to make the ball 'die' at the hole. The practice method I have used for learning this has been to place two pieces of light string parallel to each other and six inches apart. Then I putt from about three or four feet away, first to one end, then the other, using about six to eight balls. You will be surprised at how inept you are when you first try this type of practice and how expert you become after you have worked on it for a few weeks.

"Another interesting practice technique is to blindfold yourself and putt to a glass tumbler from about three feet away. Put the blindfold up on your forehead while you 'square' yourself to the ball and your intended line. Then lower the blindfold and putt away. This is wonderful practice for helping you visualize a square-blade position in your backswing and also to help you rid yourself of any tendency to look up. With nothing to see, and merely the sound of the ball hitting the tumbler to guide you, there is no temptation to look up or to move your head as you hit the ball."

But surely golf's foremost spokesman for the value of carpet putting is Dr. Peter Cranford of Augusta, Georgia, a practicing psychologist who has studied golf and golfers with the same thoroughness and intensity that his professional colleagues study other phases of human behavior. For his experiment to determine the value of carpet putting, he hit and recorded 5,000 carpet putts and an equal number on a practice putting green. These are his general conclusions:

"The chief value of practicing on a carpet is to standardize the grip, stance, and stroke so that the ball will roll straight. This is best undertaken on a uniform rug so that our observation may be more accurate.

"Carpet putting should be practiced only until you are reasonably sure that the swing will 'repeat,' as modern lingo has it. It will also be of value for sinking short and uncomplicated putts.

"However, there are comparatively few uncomplicated putts, and the more difficult ones must be learned on the greens. It is only by practicing on greens that one learns to putt on greens."

One point on which nearly all the experts agree is

that putting practice sessions should last only for as long as the player can give his full attention to the matter at hand. They theorize that if you lose your concentration and start hitting practice putts carelessly, you will tend to do the same in actual play.

9. Rules

A THOROUGH knowledge and proper application of the rules of golf as they apply to putting can save you a considerable number of strokes.

First, you should know exactly what the putting green is as defined in Section II of the rules of the United States Golf Association. "The 'putting green,'" says the U.S.G.A., "is all ground of the hole being played which is specially prepared for putting or otherwise defined as such by the Committee." The area just off the putting green, which is generally known as the fringe, or apron, of the green, is not considered under the rules to be part of the putting green.

You should know, for instance, that if your ball is on the fringe of the green you may not clean it or otherwise touch it. Many courses have adopted a local rule that you may spot the ball and pick it up to clean it—once, and only once—for your first putt after the ball is on the putting green proper. Also, you can move the ball to avoid casual water intervening between your ball and the hole only if your ball is on the putting green, not when your ball is on the fringe.

The penalties for having your ball strike the pin (loss of hole in match play; two strokes in stroke [medal] play) apply only if your ball is on the putting green. If your ball is on the fringe, or anywhere else off the putting green, you may leave the pin in the hole as a possible backstop in case you hit the ball too hard. (Some golfers consider it an advantage to have the pin in the hole; others do not, assuming that the hole can be seen easily with the pin out. This is another matter of personal preference. On a downhill shot from just off the green, where the problem is to keep the ball from running too far past the hole, you probably would want the pin left in the hole. On a level or uphill shot, where making the ball stop quickly enough is not a problem, you probably would want the pin taken out or attended. That is the way the majority of the pros handle the situation.)

When you are on the putting green, you should have the pin removed or attended so that it can be removed as soon as you hit your putt. The penalties for having your ball strike the pin from a position on the putting green are too severe to warrant taking a chance, and they apply even though the ball goes in the hole.

A most helpful rule to know in putting is the one concerning casual water on the putting green. By U.S.G.A. definition, casual water "is any temporary accumulation of water which is visible before or after the player takes his stance and which is not a hazard of itself or is not in a water hazard. Snow and ice are 'casual water' unless otherwise determined by Local Rule."

Off the putting green, the player's ball must be in casual water, or the casual water must interfere with the player's stance or stroke, before he is entitled to a free drop under the rules. But the casual water rule goes further in regard to the putting green.

"On the putting green, . . . if such conditions [casual water] intervene between a ball lying on the putting green and the hole, the player may lift the ball and place it without penalty in the nearest position to where it lay which affords maximum relief from these conditions, but not nearer the hole."

Thus you don't have to putt either out of casual water or through it. The latter point is frequently misunderstood or overlooked. But you may putt through casual water, as you might elect to do if you have a long approach putt and the casual water is concentrated in a small area near the hole. Then you can feel free to hit the ball plenty hard, counting on the accumulation of water near the hole to slow your ball down and stop it near the cup. (You cannot, however, lift out of casual water and choose a putting line where more casual water intervenes between your ball and the hole. If you take your privileges under a rule, you must carry out the rule fully, not partially. You would have to go to "the nearest position from where it lay which affords maximum relief from these conditions. . . .")

Perhaps the most misunderstood rule of putting is the one that concerns a ball overhanging the lip of the cup. One issue is how long the player who hit the ball can wait to see if the ball is still moving and will eventually fall in. The other is what that player's opponent, or, in the case of stroke play, his fellow competitor, can do about the situation.

Many golfers think that the rules permit the player to wait a specified length of time to see if the ball will fall in—five minutes, or three minutes, or thirty seconds, or the like. This is not so.

"When any part of the ball overhangs the edge of the hole," says Rule 35-lh, "the owner of the ball is not allowed more than a few seconds to determine whether it is at rest (not moving). If by then the ball has not fallen into the hole, it is deemed to be at rest. Penalty for breach of rule:Match play—loss of hole; stroke play—two strokes."

In match play, the player's opponent may, after "a

few seconds" have elapsed, concede the next stroke and "may remove the opponent's ball with a club or otherwise." In stroke play a fellow competitor may request that the ball be putted out or spotted, and if the player does not comply, the rule against undue delay can be invoked, and a two-stroke penalty assessed. (For repeated offenses against this rule, as might be deemed to have occurred if the player stubbornly insisted on leaving the ball there to see if it would fall in, the penalty is disqualification.)

Far too many golfers seem to be unfamiliar with, or simply ignore, the rule concerning touching the line of a putt. Some even go so far as to use their feet to press down the grass along the line of their putt—a gross violation of the rule. Others do the same job with the bottom of their putters.

The rule states that the line of the putt must not be touched except to repair an indentation left by a ball hitting on the green, to remove a loose impediment, or to mark the ball for cleaning. The player may, however, place the club in front of the ball in addressing it so long as he does not press anything down. Penalty for breach of this rule: Match play—loss of hole; medal play—two strokes.

It should be noted that the rule does allow the repair of ball marks and the removal of loose impediments, as follows:

"The player may repair damage to the putting green

caused by the impact of a ball. The ball may be lifted to permit such repair and shall be replaced on the spot from which it was lifted; in match play the ball must be replaced immediately if the opponent so requests. If a ball be moved during such repair, it shall be replaced without penalty.

"The player may move any loose impediment on the putting green by picking it up or brushing it aside with his hand or a club without pressing anything down. If the ball be moved, it shall be replaced without penalty." The rule adds that spike marks on the green may not be repaired. The rules also state, "During the play of a hole, a player shall not test the surface of the putting green by rolling a ball or roughening or scraping the surface."

Some golfers may benefit by availing themselves of their privileges under the rule which permits the player's partner, or his caddy, or his partner's caddy, to advise him on and indicate how much a putt is apt to break. The rule states:

"When the player's ball is on the putting green, the player's caddie, his partner or his partner's caddie may, before the stroke is played, point out a line for putting, but the line of the putt may not be touched in front of, to the side of, or behind the hole. No mark shall be placed anywhere on the putting green to indicate a line for putting." Thus the helper may indicate the line by holding the head of a club to one side of the hole or the other, as long as he does not touch the club-head to the ground.

Two seldom invoked, but nevertheless important, rules prohibit the removal of a previously unattended flagstick while a ball is in motion, or the spotting and picking up of another ball while a ball is in motion. You are also forbidden to putt while an opponent's or fellow competitor's ball is in motion. The usual loss of hole (match play) and two-stroke (stroke play) penalties apply in the above situations.

In match play particularly, it is important to know your rights and obligations pertaining to the marking and lifting of a ball. Here is the rule governing match plays:

" 'A' alone can determine whether 'B's' ball shall be lifted while 'A' plays. When the ball nearer the hole lies on the putting green, if the player considers that the opponent's ball might interfere with his play, the player may require the opponent to lift his ball, without penalty. If the player's ball stops on the spot formerly occupied by the lifted ball, the player shall first play another stroke before the lifted ball is replaced. If the player's ball be touched accidentally or moved in complying with this Rule, no penalty shall be incurred and the ball if moved shall be replaced. (Penalty for breach: loss of hole.)"

To put it another way: the player whose turn it is to shoot has control over whether his opponent's ball shall be lifted or left where it is. If, for instance, you were putting and your opponent's ball lay just beyond the hole from your position, the logical strategy would be to leave the ball there possibly to stop your ball if it went by the cup. But if your opponent's ball lay close to the cup on your side, you would want to have it lifted, because if your ball hit his and knocked it in, he would "be deemed to have holed out with his last stroke." In any case, if your ball hits your opponent's and moves it, he has the option of replacing it or leaving it where your ball knocked it.

In stroke play, the business of one ball's interfering with or assisting the play of another is handled a bit differently. In substance the rule states that the player may not only have a fellow competitor's ball lifted or played out if he thinks it may interfere with his play, but also a fellow competitor may have a ball lifted or played out if he thinks it may assist another player.

In connection with lifting, the prescribed way to mark a ball's position is by placing an object, such as a small coin, immediately behind the ball; if the object interferes with another player, it should be moved one or more putterhead lengths to one side.

The major rule change in 1966 had to do with striking an unattended flagstick (pin). The change provided, "No prohibition against striking in play from off putting green within 20 yards of hole. (Striking unattended flagstick prohibited only when ball is played from putting green.)"

The Rules Committee also authorized local committees to adopt local rules to the following effect:

"Saving Time on Putting Green: 1. Stroke Play—Each player plays continuously until he holes out; however, fellow-competitor may request him to lift to avoid standing on fellow-competitor's line of putt. Match Play and Stroke Play—Ball may be lifted for cleaning purposes only before the first putt. Cleaning may be done incidentally when ball is lifted under other Rules."

10. *Highlights and Anecdotes*

THE history of golf has been written, so to speak, on the putting greens. In any session of locker-room reminiscences you will find that perhaps 90 percent of the stories told will center on putts—long putts made, short putts missed, and an array of oddities that well nigh defy belief. Every avid golfer, it seems, has his own favorite putting story.

In the opinion of most golf historians, the most spectacular clutch putting drama in golf history was staged by Jerry Barber on the seventieth, seventy-first, and seventy-second holes of the 1961 PGA Championship at Olympia Fields Country Club near Chicago.

Barber, a small bespectacled man who was then 45 years old and who had never won a major championship, came to the seventieth hole 4 strokes down to the leader, Don January. Dusk was beginning to envelop the golf course and many of the thousands of spectators were leaving, secure in the belief that nothing could happen to keep January from being the winner.

On the sixteenth green, Barber curled in a 20-footer for a birdie 3. It took him 2 wood shots to reach the par-4 seventeenth, and he was 40 feet from the cup. He knocked in the putt for another birdie 3.

Now there was new excitement. Spectators began telling each other that if Barber could get his long-iron second shot fairly close on the par-4 eighteenth he just might make the putt and get a tie, since January had played the last 3 holes in 1 over par and his once-comfortable margin was now down to a single stroke.

But Barber's second shot came to rest on the left part of the green and the cup was set on the right portion. The distance was not less than 60 feet, and there were perhaps a half a dozen subtle breaks between Barber's ball and the hole. Again the spectators conceded the championship to January.

It was very nearly dark as Barber lined up the putt and took his stance for his last desperate effort to tie. He stroked the ball briskly, and several seconds later saw it disappear into the cup. He had his miraculous tie. The next day he shot a 67 in the playoff to beat January by a stroke.

The putt that had perhaps the greatest effect on the history of golf was made on the seventy-second hole of the 1929 National Open at the Winged Foot Club in

Mamaroneck, New York. The length of the putt has been generally estimated at 12 feet. Bobby Jones made it to tie with Al Espinosa, to whom he had lost a 4-stroke lead on the 3 preceding holes. Some say the ball barely toppled in the side of the hole. Others say it went dead center. In any event, it gave Jones the tie. He won the 36-hole playoff the following day by 23 strokes.

The great significance of the putt is that had Jones missed it, he might never have attempted to win his Grand Slam of 1930. He latter confided this to some friends. "If I'd missed that putt and lost a tournament already won," Jones told Grantland Rice, "I hate to think of what might have happened to my confidence. And without confidence a golfer is little more than a hacker."

One of golf's most famous putts was a 6-footer that was never struck at all. It was conceded to Bobby Cruickshank by Al Watrous in the 1932 PGA Championship at the Keller Course in St. Paul, Minnesota. At the time, Watrous was 9 up with 13 holes to play in their 36-hole match. A miss by Cruickshank would have left Watrous 10 up with 12 to play, since Cruickshank's putt was for a par and a tie on the hole. Watrous gave him the putt.

"I had built up a satisfying lead of five up at the end of the first eight holes, and I had increased my lead to nine up with thirteen to play. The sixth hole is a short par-three, and Bobby missed the green. I hit the corner of the green with my tee shot. Bobby chipped by the cup about six feet above the hole. I putted up close and Bobby conceded my second putt for a par three.

"A little bit earlier, Bobby had mentioned to me that this was the worst beating he ever had, and since I was nine up at the time, I would be going ten up if he missed the putt. Feeling a bit sorry for him and not wanting him to go down in double figures, I conceded him the putt. I can remember so clearly that we passed a man who had been lying on a bank of the next tee and saw the play on the sixth green.

"As I went by the man, I heard him say to another person near him, 'He shouldn't have conceded that putt. He might be sorry for that.' Whether Bobby heard it, too, I don't know. Perhaps he did.

"Anyway, I was still nine up and playing the seventh hole with only twelve to go. Bobby holed a twenty-footer for a birdie on the seventh while I missed an eight-footer. I was then eight up. Bobby won the eighth hole with a par.

"The ninth hole is a long four-par and we were both on in two. I was away and three-putted while Bobby took two putts and was only six down.

"I still remember the change in attitude of both of us as we went to the tenth tee. Earlier we had been discussing Bobby's chances of getting a job at one of the Detroit district courses and how I could help him.

"Suddenly Bobby was all business and friendliness

went out the window. He could sense that he was back in the match.

"I won't tell you what happened hole by hole, because it was simply disastrous for me. I played well but Bobby played, and particularly putted, sensationally. On eighteen straight holes after the famous conceded putt, Bobby had eleven one-putts. One of them was a seventy-footer on the fifteenth. Another hole we halved in birdies. But coming to the eighteenth I was still one up and Bobby had played the back nine in six under par. He knocked in another long putt for a birdie at eighteen. We were in overtime and the big lead I had was all gone.

"The first, second, and third extra holes were tied, although twice I had the chance to roll in the winning putt. The story of the fourth hole, I think, is funny enough, looking back at it now, to retell in more detail.

"The fourth hole at Keller is a short hole, probably about a hundred and forty yards. Bobby hit his tee shot over the green and up a bank behind it.

"Cruickshank was still outside my ball in two. He putted again, and missed, and was outside of me in three. Bobby was definitely in for a four at best and I hadn't taken my second shot yet. He was just about to shake hands with me but decided not to and knocked his putt in for a four. My putt was a delicate downhill putt on a very close-shaven green and I didn't want to leave it short. I didn't. I went past the hole not more than a foot. I thought Bobby was going to concede my putt, but he didn't and I proceeded to putt my one-footer too delicately. Needless to say, we had tied in bogeys. I had three-putted from two feet away.

"The next hole was the last in the overtime. Bobby holed another six-footer, making his par. I was on the green in two, putted too strongly, went by the cup and missed a three-footer coming back. Cruickshank had won an 'impossible-to-win' watch. My advice to you is, 'Don't ever concede your opponent a putt—not even a two-incher.' "

Another putt that affected the history of golf, most tragically so for the man who struck it, came on the fifth hole of the Augusta National Club during the first round of the 1962 Masters Tournament. Dow Finster-wald had just missed a short putt on this green and was walking to the sixth tee. In a thoughtless moment, he dropped a ball near the edge of the green and stroked it a few feet with his putter—not even in the direction of the hole. Dow was assessed a 2-stroke penalty for practicing on the green, which was clearly against the rules under which the Masters was being played. He was tied with Arnold Palmer and Gary Player with 280 at the end of the regulation 72 holes. He lost in the playoff. Without the penalty, theoretically at least, he would have won the tournament by 2 strokes.

A missed putt of only 30½ inches on the final hole

A happy Lew Worsham acepted the 1947 U.S. Open trophy after Sam Snead missed a 30½-inch putt that would have kept the tournament alive. Despite his fantastic golf record, Snead has yet to win a U.S. Open tournament.

of the playoff with Lew Worsham cost Sam Snead the 1947 National Open at the St. Louis (Missouri) Country Club. When Snead missed this one, Worsham made his from 29½ inches for the championship. Had Snead gotten the putt down, he would have kept the playoff alive. Instead he lost 69–70.

They had been all even coming to the final green, with Worsham 40 feet from the flag on the apron of the green in 2. Snead was on in 2, 15 feet away. Worsham chipped just by the cup, almost holing the shot. Snead's first putt stopped short.

Assuming he was still out, Snead walked up to stroke his short second putt, but Worsham, evidently feeling that he might be away, asked for a measurement to determine whose turn it was to putt. The tape showed the distances noted above. Snead putted and missed. Worsham tapped his in. Another chapter in the history of golf had been written on a green.

The great Walter Hagen, like Arnold Palmer in a later time, settled many an issue with a sensational putt.

One of Hagen's most sensational putts was made late in a PGA Championship match against Leo Diegel in the 1920's at Olympia Fields near Chicago.

Diegel and Hagen were playing in the quarter-finals of the tournament. Hagen had been behind throughout the round as they came to the seventeenth hole. Walter was 2 down (2 holes behind in match play) with

During the "Roaring '20s" Walter Hagen was literally the King of Golf. His ability with a putter was the downfall of many of his opponents.

just 2 holes left to play. If Diegel won the seventeenth hole, it was all over for Hagen.

The seventeenth at Olympia Fields requires 2 great golf shots to reach the green. Hagen's second shot was beautifully placed hole-high about 15 feet to the left of the pin. Diegel's second shot went into a ditch and his third left his ball on the green, but 40 feet from the hole. Hagen figured Diegel for 2 putts and a 5 on the hole. But, much to his amazement, Diegel put his 40-footer in the middle of the cup for a par 4. That meant Hagen had to get a 3 to win the hole and stay alive in the tournament. He had to sink his 15-foot putt.

His putting line was tough. He realized that the contour of the green went sharply downhill to the hole. He figured he had to stop the forward progress of the ball so as to allow the ball to pick up its own momentum and roll into the cup. He also knew he had to hit the cup dead center because the momentum would carry the ball past the cup if there was any margin of error.

But Walter Hagen, being the great professional he was, didn't seem to be worried. He stepped up to the ball, sighted his shot, and putted—dead center into the hole. The seventeenth was his.

The shock of losing the hole because of such an extraordinary pressure putt had a disastrous effect on Leo Diegel's game. He lost the eighteenth hole and was ultimately eliminated by Hagen from the tournament.

Perhaps the single best-known putt ever made at the Masters Tournament was Cary Middlecoff's 80-footer for an eagle 3 on the par-5 thirteenth hole. It put Middlecoff 7 under par for the round at that point, and the 65 he shot that day gave him a 4-shot lead that he later increased to win the 1955 Masters by a then record 7-stroke margin over Ben Hogan and Sam Snead. Cary remembers it this way:

"In the second round of the Masters Tournament, I came to the thirteenth hole five under par. On this famous par-five hole my second shot with a three-wood hit on the green about pin-high and rolled about eighty feet past the cup, way on the back of this long green. As I looked over the tremendously long putt, I could only think how nice it would be to get it close to the hole for an easy birdie and go six under par. There were several slight undulations between my ball and the cup, but otherwise it was a level putt with just a small amount of left break.

"I decided that the best way to get the ball close was to try as hard as I could to hole it out. When the ball left my putter, I knew I had hit a good putt, and I watched it roll through the little dips in the happy knowledge that it would probably stop no more than a foot or two away, making for an easy birdie. The ball still had about twenty feet to go when I saw and sensed that it might go in. The gallery sensed the same thing when the ball was about fifteen feet short, and a tenta-

Cary Middlecoff ran away from the rest of the field when he won the 1955 Masters tournament. The highlight of his performance was a fabulous 65 over the Augusta National course in the second round. During that round he sank an 80-foot putt on the par-5 thirteenth for an eagle three.

tive cheer went up. At five feet short, I could see that the ball was rolling at just the right speed and that it was dead in the middle of the cup. And then 'plop,' an eagle three.

"That was about as big a thrill as I have ever received from golf, and several in the big gallery told me it was one of their biggest golf thrills."

Some putts are long remembered because of their tragicomic qualities. Bill Hyndman, the fine amateur, had one from about 40 feet on the eleventh green at the Augusta National during the 1959 Masters. The pin was in the back left corner of the green, perhaps 12 to 15 feet from the edge of the water hazard that fronts this green. Hyndman's putt was over a sort of hog-back, or ridge, and he knew that if it got on the left side of the ridge it would keep breaking left away from the hole.

But Hyndman was a mite careless and let the ball move a touch too far to the left. And it kept on breaking left—right off the green and into the water. He had to go back to the drop area, leaving the hazard between him and the hole. He wound up with a 7 on a hole where he had putted for a birdie 3.

Hyndman's playing partner was Lloyd Mangrum, who was always a man to speak his mind. "Bill," said Mangrum, "that was the dumbest putt I ever saw."

A putt that Lawson Little could never forget was made by his amateur partner on the last hole of a pro-amateur tournament at the Seminole Club in Florida in 1949. That was before the golf authorities began to frown so heavily on Calcutta pools in connection with tournaments, and there was a tremendous one for this tournament at this very rich club. Little himself stood to win some $12,500 if his team finished ahead of the rest.

Little and partner came to the last hole needing only a par 4 to win, and the amateur's handicap gave him a stroke on the hole. A bogey would give him a net par and the victory. The amateur hit 2 fine shots to the edge of the green and seemed assured of a regulation par, which would mean a net birdie. Little, meanwhile, had hit a poor drive and only a fair second shot, so he picked up on the hole so he could give his full attention to advising his partner.

The amateur hit his first putt some 3 feet short, leaving a simple uphill putt for his par. It was all they could have wished, and Little congratulated him on his strategy, cautioning him at the same time to just tap the next one up within an inch or two of the cup for a cinch bogey.

The amateur did tap his second putt to within an inch of the hole. But, as Little stood by in horror, the man reached out with his putter and raked the ball back toward him. Little's anguished cry came too late. The amateur jumped aside and the ball trickled on down to the lower edge of the green. And since the ball had never been holed, the man lay 5 at that point. He took 3 more putts for an 8 on the hole, by which time their Calcutta pool prize had shrunk by several thousand dollars. The amateur, being accustomed to match play and having those very short putts conceded to him, had simply forgotten, in the excitement of being about to win the tournament, to hole the bogey putt as called for in the rules of stroke play.

It is a well-known fact that golfers go for gimmicks. Let them see another player, particularly a professional, succeeding with something out of the ordinary, and soon they will be trying the same thing. So it was that when Joe Turnesa won the Metropolitan Open putting one-handed some years ago, the New York area golfing landscape was soon dotted with players trying the one-handed gimmick. Chances are that some of them stayed with this technique after Turnesa himself discarded it.

The same sort of thing undoubtedly happened after Sam Snead putted on the last few holes of the 1966 PGA Tournament with his own outlandish version of the croquet-style putting stroke. Snead straddled the line of his putts, as the croquet putters do, and gripped the shaft with his right hand just a few inches above the clubhead. And on the last hole there at the Firestone Country Club in Akron, Ohio, with the finish of the tournament being shown on national television, Snead holed a tough 15-footer.

However, much as the golfing public did not realize

that Snead had resorted to this method in desperation. His 54-year-old nerves had become so jumpy that a couple of times in the early stages of the last round he had, with his normal putting stroke, inadvertently hit the ball twice with the same swing. That was why he adopted the strange style that the television audience saw him use on the final holes.

Bobby Cruickshank once came up with a theory that the best way to putt was to keep one eye on the ball and the other on the hole—a difficult feat, but, so Cruickshank thought at first, the answer to the problem of putting. He did fine with it for the first two rounds in a tournament in the Carolinas, but in the third round he almost missed the ball altogether a couple of times. And more than once he hit the ball twice with the same stroke. Reluctantly he went back to the more prosaic method of looking at the back of the ball when making his stroke.

Many golfers have theorized that the best way to putt is to look at the hole (with both eyes) rather than at the ball, just as hunters look at the target rather than at the end of the barrel where the ammunition will come out. This theory applied to putting, has also proved false many times.

There have been some outlandish but effective putting tools invented as well, only to be declared illegal by the U.S.G.A. Phil Rodgers once tried out a putter with a ball-and-socket arrangement at the top of the shaft, which allowed the top of the putter to be held stationary with the left hand while the lower part was being manipulated with the right hand. But the authorities cited the rule against the club's having any moving parts. Rodgers went back to trying to achieve the same general effect with the split grip he now uses.

An ingenious Californian once devised a putter whose shaft branched out into 2 handles at the point where the grip normally starts. By using a kind of pumping action stroke, he could putt with this contraption like a magician. But he couldn't bypass the rule that says the grip of the club must be a (single) continuation of the shaft, and must be generally straight.

Cotton Hill, a professional in Shreveport, Louisiana, actually prefers to putt with his sand wedge, and he is very good with it. A few years ago in a tournament he startled the spectators, and perhaps cast a little doubt on his sanity, by using his putter to roll the ball up the bank of a green to within about 5 feet of the hole. Then he used his wedge to make the putt.

Some golfers think that using the putter from off the green, except from just off the putting surface in the fringe, is something the big-name pros would never do. But Jack Nicklaus did it on a most important shot in the 1965 Masters. Jack's second shot on the seventy-second hole was some 20 feet off the green to the left, on ground packed hard by spectators during the week of the tournament. He needed to get down in 3 shots from there to win the tournament.

Looking for the safest shot possible to get the ball on the green within easy 2-putt distance, Nicklaus chose the putter. He rolled the ball up the bank of the green to within about 5 feet of the hole. He knocked the next one in to win by 2 shots.

A number of golfers hit their shots right-handed and their putts left-handed. Some play left-handed until they reach the green and then putt right-handed. A noted Tennessee amateur of some years back named Tom White putted his long putts right-handed and his short putts left-handed. But none of these switch putters are to be found among the big names of golf.

Finally we come to what the editors of this book nominate as the strangest putt and the strangest non-putt in the history of golf.

The strangest putt was hit by Ky Laffoon, a ranking pro of the 1930's and the early 1940's, who was part Indian and known to his fellow pros as "The Chief." The Chief was noted for his excellent golf game in general and for his "quail-high" iron shots in particular. He was even more noted for the shortness and intensity of his temper. He came to the last hole in a North Carolina tournament needing to get down in 2 putts from 3 feet to win top money. He hit his first putt in what he considered to be exactly the way it should have been hit, but it lipped out of the hole and stopped a couple of inches away. He needed only to tap the little one in to be the winner. But when the well-hit putt lipped out on the Chief, he grew angry. Instead of tapping in the 2 incher, he reached out with his putter and brought the clubhead down hard on top of the ball. Had he hit just a small fraction to either side, he would have knocked it all the way off the green. Fortunately, he hit it flush on top. The ball jumped 2 feet in the air and dropped straight down into the hole.

The story of the nonputt is part of the lore of the Memphis (Tennessee) Country Club and is vouched for by a large number of veteran members who saw it happen. One of the club's best golfers, Hunter Phillips, was playing in the finals of the club tournament. He came to the last hole one down and had a 3-foot putt on the eighteenth green to square the match and take it into extra holes. His 3-footer was a tough little breaking putt. Mr. Phillips surveyed it at some length from all four sides. Twice he stepped up to hit it, then backed away to look again at the line. Finally, he reached down and picked up the ball, and shook hands with his opponent.

"You got the match," he said. "No way I could make that thing."

Index